Baptism
and
Belonging

Baptism and Belonging

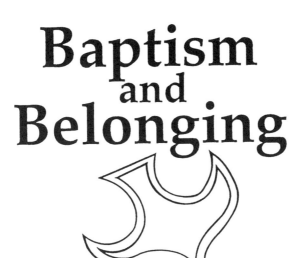

A Resource for Christian Worship

Prepared for use of the
Christian Church (Disciples of Christ)

by

The Division of Homeland Ministries

Edited by Keith Watkins

Contributors

LaTaunya M. Bynum
Michael K. Kinnamon
Margaret A. Lowe
Peter M. Morgan
Stephen V. Sprinkle

Chalice Press
St. Louis, Missouri

© Copyright 1991 Chalice Press

Cover design: Kathleen A. Bromm

Library of Congress Cataloging–in–Publication Data

Baptism and belonging / edited by Keith Watkins.
Includes texts of baptismal liturgies, including those proposed by the Consultation on Christian Union.
1. Baptism—Christian Church (Disciples of Christ) 2. Christian Church (Disciples of Christ)—Doctrines. 3. Christian Church (Disciples of Christ)—Liturgy. 4. Baptism and church membership. I. Watkins, Keith. II. Consultation on Christian Union. Christian baptism 1991.
BX7325.5.B3B36 1991   261'.16   91-25312
ISBN 0-8272-0219-9

Printed in the United States of America

TABLE OF CONTENTS

PREFACE   viii

THE RENEWAL OF CHRISTIAN BAPTISM AND CHRISTIAN
       COMMUNITY   1

PART ONE: Baptism

THE DISCIPLES VISION OF CHRISTIAN BAPTISM   15

    Rites and Texts   25
        A. The Invitation   25
        B. Confession of Faith   26
        C. Rededication of Faith or Renewal of
            Baptismal Vows   26
        D. Transfer of Membership from Another
            Congregation   27
        E. Baptism   28

ECUMENICAL SERVICES OF BAPTISM   31

    Rites and Texts   37
        Rite One   37
        Rite Two   42

BAPTISM IN SPECIAL CIRCUMSTANCES   51

    The Service in Outline   55
    Rites and Texts   56
        A. For Someone Critically Ill   56
        B. For an Infant in Critical Condition   57
        C. For a Wheelchair-Bound Person   60
        D. For Someone Confined   62
        E. Congregational Affirmation of the Newly Baptized   63

THE EASTER VIGIL   **67**

    Outline and Description of the Service   **67**
    Order for the Great Vigil of Easter   **69**
        Service of Light   **70**
        Service of the Word   **76**
        Service of Water   **80**
        Service of the Bread and Cup   **85**

PART TWO: Belonging

BELONGING   **91**

    When Life Begins   **94**
    Thanksgiving for the Birth or Adoption of a Child   **98**
    Affirmation of the Baptismal Covenant   **102**

BECOMING FAITHFUL...BECOMING CHRISTIAN   **109**

    Rites and Texts
        Stage One: Introduction to the Christian Community   **113**
        Stage Two: Candidacy for Baptism   **115**
        Stage Three: Incorporation into Christ   **122**

PART THREE: Essays

CHILDREN AND CHRISTIAN BAPTISM   **125**

EASTER AND THE CELEBRATION OF BAPTISM   **131**

TRADITION, AUTHORITY, AND THE BAPTISMAL
    FORMULA   **140**

NOTES   **147**

PREFACE

Baptism and Belonging contains instructions, prayers, and other liturgical texts for Christian baptism, the reception of children, and the affirmation of baptismal vows. It also provides descriptions and liturgical texts for the Easter Vigil and an extended program of nurture and worship that prepares people for baptism into Christ and life in the church. The final portion of this book is a group of essays on topics related to baptismal practice in the church.

The rites and texts draw upon several sources including publications of the Consultation on Church Union, traditional practices of the Christian Church (Disciples of Christ), and contemporary adaptations of ancient Christian practice. Some of the materials have been newly composed for this book; and all previously published inclusions have been edited for the purposes of this volume.

Baptism and Belonging is addressed primarily to congregations of the Christian Church (Disciples of Christ). However, all of the liturgies and most of the introductions and essays may also be useful to people in other churches. Noteworthy in this regard are:

The COCU liturgies here published for the first time in one volume.

Liturgical materials for baptism in special circumstances, such as the baptism of a newborn child near death.

A new adaptation of the Rite of Christian Initiation of Adults.

Orders for celebrating baptism when the candidates are not able to speak on their own behalf.

With appreciation, the editorial team acknowledges the following sources of previously published texts and services and offers thanks for permission to reprint edited versions of these materials: the Consultation on Church Union; *Book of Worship:United Church of Christ; Worship for the Way* (Presbyterian Church in Canada); and the

Council on Christian Unity of the Christian Church (Disciples of Christ).

The following writers contributed liturgical texts and essays for this book, and their work is gratefully acknowledged:

Stephen V. Sprinkle: essay and liturgical texts concerning the Disciples vision of Christian baptism;

Michael K. Kinnamon: essay on children and Christian baptism and basic authorship of "Christian Baptism Rite Two";

LaTaunya M. Bynum: essay on baptism in special circumstances;

Peter M. Morgan: essay on Easter and the celebration of baptism and edited liturgy for the Easter Vigil;

Margaret A. Lowe: "Becoming Faithful...Becoming Christian";

Keith Watkins: introductory essays, liturgical texts, and essay on the baptismal formula.

The Division of Homeland Ministries has developed *Baptism and Belonging* to add to a previous volume of worship resources of the Christian Church (Disciples of Christ). *Thankful Praise: A Resource for Christian Worship* (CBP Press 1987) presents materials for the Sunday service of the Word and Lord's Supper.

Keith Watkins has served as general editor and principal writer of *Baptism and Belonging*. Watkins, a scholar in the field of worship, is the Herald B. Monroe Professor of Practical Parish Ministry and director of Sweeney Chapel, Christian Theological Seminary, Indianapolis. In addition to writing one of the units, Margaret A. Lowe helped to shape the project in its developing phase. Proxida Jackson has done the word processing with zest and skill. Herbert H. Lambert, as former editor of CBP Press, and his successor David P. Polk, have encouraged the editorial team in the developing of this book.

In addition to the above-named participants, a group of reviewers has responded to successive drafts of portions of this book. Their contributions are gratefully acknowledged:

James H. Benton
Colbert S. Cartwright
Linda L. Chenoweth
Anthony L. Dunnavant
Michael G. Fitch
John D. Grabner

Lucile Long Hair
Paul H. Jones
Larry B. Metzger
Nancy Claire Pittman
David P. Polk
Norman Reed
William B. Rose-Heim

Baptism and Belonging is by the church, for the church, and to the glory of God.

Peter M. Morgan, Managing Editor
Director of Worship and Renewal
Division of Homeland Ministries

THE RENEWAL OF CHRISTIAN BAPTISM AND CHRISTIAN COMMUNITY

In churches around the world Christian baptism is undergoing significant change. For generations Christians have been deeply divided in their understandings of the "one baptism" (Ephesians 4:5); and their ways of conducting this rite have varied widely. Now a new consensus is emerging about what baptism means. Although sharply contrasting modes of baptism continue in practice, the mood surrounding this variety is being significantly altered by the growing agreement among the churches about what happens when people are baptized into Christ Jesus.

One evidence of this change is expressed in architecture as churches that formerly baptized by sprinkling or pouring replace bowl-sized baptismal fonts with pools large enough to immerse adults. Published texts for the baptismal service also show the change. Formerly brief and oriented toward the baptism of infants, new services are longer, fuller, and designed with adults as the primary candidates. Theological writings are another evidence of the transformation. They have largely set aside the long-standing debates over the mode of baptism and the relationship between faith and divine initiative. Now theologies of baptism stress classical themes of the meaning of baptism and recommend that the form of the rite express those meanings as fully as possible. The radical shift in Catholic and Protestant churches can be summed up in these few lines:

> The baptism of adults is once again understood to be the theological norm for all aspects of Christian initiation. Other patterns and practices are now being restated and reshaped in the light of this recovered theological principle.[1]

This transformation of baptism is more than a revision of rites and ceremonies. It promises to create enlivened churches where people experience forgiveness, receive power, and are called to faithful life in the world. The reform of baptism and the renewal of the church go hand in hand.

1

Importance to Disciples

This renewal of interest in baptism is especially important to the Christian Church (Disciples of Christ). In the early years of our history, baptism for the remission of sins was central to our message. This doctrine distinguished us from other churches, was the source of much of the vitality of Disciples life, and anchored our sacramental life in the classical Christian tradition. Baptism for the remission of sins was integral to the doctrine of conversion that Alexander Campbell presented in his writings and that became the basis for evangelistic outreach by Disciples for generations thereafter. This doctrine of conversion, said William Robinson, is the most important contribution of the Disciples to the ecumenical discussion.[2]

Even with this strong baptismal heritage, however, baptismal theology and practice among Disciples are less vigorous than once was the case. Although our normal practice continues to be the immersion of penitent believers, the theology supporting the practice is often muted. Furthermore, the immersion itself is often conducted with little more ceremony than the reciting of the confession of faith from Matthew 16 and the trinitarian formula of Matthew 28. Thus the expressive power of a fuller baptismal liturgy is often not experienced by those baptized or by congregations. By participating in the new discussions concerning baptism, Disciples can recover the strength of our own tradition and witness to it in our ecumenical relationships.

This renaissance of interest in baptism is important to Disciples for another reason. As the decades have passed by, challenging theological and pastoral questions have emerged in our church. Some have to do with the relationship between baptism and church membership, some with the relationship of baptism and the Lord's Supper, and some with the relationship between baptism and salvation. These questions begin not as scholarly debates over theology but as problems in daily life. People still ask what they must do to be saved. They still seek a gracious and loving God. They desire to become part of a community that cares for them and challenges them to live life to its fullest potential. Parents have to decide how to respond when their unbaptized children reach for the bread and grape juice as the trays pass by on Sunday mornings. These questions from the human heart are at the center of the church's practices of baptism and belonging. The rediscovery of classical baptism teaching and practice will help Disciples, as well as people in other church traditions, meet the religious needs of the people who come to our churches seeking the grace of God. The ecumenical framework of discussions can assist pastors, boards of elders, and the people of our churches as together they seek to find their way through the maze of questions related to baptism and belonging to Christ and the church.

The Recovery of the Classic Theology of Baptism

One of the most important aspects of the modern transformation of baptism is the recovery of biblical and theological understandings of the classical doctrine of Christian baptism. For several generations theologians and other church scholars have been reexamining sacramental practice and theology. Previously the main concentration was upon the celebration of the Lord's Supper, but in recent decades new attention has been given to Christian baptism. This classical doctrine of baptism can be summarized around six headings.

Participation in the death and resurrection of Jesus Christ. The classic text for this idea is Romans 6:1–11. Here Paul proclaims that by baptism we "have been buried" with Christ "into death" and are raised with him to "walk in newness of life." Baptism by immersion is a powerful sign of this radical change of life. Even more powerful is the idea itself—that in the watery grave God claims our life and as we rise up out of the water God gives it back to us transformed after the likeness of Jesus Christ.

The washing of regeneration. Although the metaphor is different, this second motif in the classical baptismal doctrine is fully harmonious with the first. In the Revised Standard Version, the phrase "washing of regeneration" appears in Titus 3:5 where this washing is coupled with renewal in the Holy Spirit, which God pours out upon us through Jesus Christ our Savior. The idea also appears in other places such as Acts 22:16 and Hebrews 10:22. The idea is also implicit in Jesus' conversation with Nicodemus in John 3. Through water and the Spirit, one is born anew, which is what the word regeneration means. The New Revised Standard Version brings these ideas out into the open with its translation of Titus 3:5: "the water of rebirth."

The forgiveness of sins. The angel's announcement to Joseph of the impending birth of Jesus included this comment: "You are to name him Jesus, for he will save his people from their sins (Matthew 1:21). Jesus preached a message of repentance and on some occasions (such as Matthew 9:2–8) forgave sins. In his sermon on Pentecost, Peter continued this theme and connected forgiveness with baptism: "Repent, and be baptized every one of you in the name of Jesus Christ so that your sins may be forgiven..." (Acts 2:38). The history of Christian theology includes extensive debate concerning the doctrines of atonement, which explain how Jesus' death works for our forgiveness; yet, the tradition of the church is unified in its conviction that baptism is intimately connected with that forgiving and saving work of Christ.

The receiving of the Holy Spirit. When Jesus was baptized, the heavens opened and the Spirit of God in the form of a dove descended upon him. Before his crucifixion, Jesus promised to send the Holy Spirit as the comforter and advocate of the disciples. On the Day of Pentecost, the Spirit came upon that small company of disciples as tongues of fire, and these followers of Jesus began to preach the gospel of their risen Lord. In the major sermon of the day, Peter instructed the people to be baptized in the name of Jesus Christ for the forgiveness of their sins. The result would be that they would receive the Holy Spirit. Ever since the Day of Pentecost, baptism has been closely identified with the indwelling presence of God's Spirit.

Incorporation into the body of Christ. An important biblical text for this baptismal motif is 1 Corinthians 12:13 where Paul affirms that by one Spirit we were all baptized into one body. The body in question is the body of Christ, the church. In Acts 2:37–42 and 9:18ff baptism precedes entry into the gathered life of the Christian community.

The sign of God's sovereignty in the world. Jesus' message combined the call to repentance and the announcement that God's commonwealth would soon come (Matthew 4:17). When he preached in the synagogue at Nazareth, he proclaimed a time when captives would be released, the blind made to see, and the oppressed set at liberty. Accounts of baptism in Acts indicate that people who were baptized began a new life that pioneered this commonwealth. In Acts 2:43ff, for example, the Jerusalem Christians created a new community of love and mutual care that expressed the spirit of the new age that Jesus had proclaimed. Although the new age has yet to come in its completeness, the community of the baptized gives a foretaste of that which is to come.

Clearly, there is nothing new about these ideas. They have been part of the church's theological tradition from the beginning, and from earliest days have been expressed in the baptismal liturgies. What has happened in recent decades is that scholars, pastors, and other church members have reflected upon these motifs and recognized again their radical character.

These understandings of Christian initiation assume something about the people being baptized: that ordinarily people old enough to speak for themselves are the appropriate candidates. The biblical accounts uniformly describe the baptism of adults. From early times children may have been baptized along with other members of their household, but at first this practice was scarcely mentioned. By the time of Augustine in the fifth century the baptism of infants had become quite common and during the next 200 years became the normal practice. Even so, the basic theological convictions that baptism is related to the forgiveness of sins and incorporation into the divine life continued to characterize baptismal rites. In recent times the implications of this underlying doctrine have been realized anew. New baptismal liturgies, while still providing for the baptism of infants, express more boldly than they used to that baptism is closely tied to faith and forgiveness.

This recovery of the classical theology of baptism has important implications for Disciples. It confirms our traditional commitment to believer's baptism as being true to scripture and to human experience. The contemporary theological scene reminds Disciples of the doctrines they have held through the years—that baptism is an action in which God transforms the one baptized; and that the baptismal candidate effectively obeys God. The result, according to traditional Disciples theology and to the classical view, is that something really happens when people are baptized. As Peter puts it in his Pentecost sermon: "Repent, and be baptized every one of you in the name of Jesus Christ so that your sins may be forgiven; and you will receive the gift of the Holy Spirit" (Acts 2:38).

A second challenge to Disciples is that we ponder the implications of what now is common practice among us. In many congregations the majority of persons baptized are pre-adolescent children from families of the church. Certainly they are able to speak for themselves; and their comprehension of the faith is greater than when they were infants. Yet to call them adults, or perhaps even believers, stretches the normal meaning of these terms as they are used outside of the church. Some have said that many congregations now practice delayed infant baptism rather than believers' baptism. The topic warrants discussion.

This recovery also challenges Disciples to be bold in expressing our baptismal doctrine. We live in an era in which large numbers of people are not participating in the Christian community. They need to understand the estrangement that marks life today and to reconceive the meaning of sin. They need to hear the good news of God in Jesus Christ. The recovery of a strong, rich baptismal theology could be the beginning of a stronger evangelistic witness than we have known for years.

Other Factors Leading to Transformation

In addition to the recovery of classical baptismal theology, three other factors have led to contemporary changes in baptismal practice. The first of these additional factors is a serious reconsideration of the place of children in the church. Are children members of the church or are they not? In most churches, both Protestant and Catholic, the practice has been to baptize children in infancy and then to delay their admission to communion until some years later. During this period of time the children are in an ambiguous state. On the one hand, they are members of the church. On the other hand, they are kept from participating in the sacrament of growth in the Christian life. The anomaly of claiming that children are members of the church but then not permitting them to participate in the church's basic life has made it necessary to open this question completely.

In churches like Disciples that baptize people old enough to speak for themselves the problem is somewhat different. During these early years the children are not considered to be members of the church. Yet they are present and participate in its public life. They sing hymns, learn to pray, and listen to sermons; ordinarily, however, they have not partaken of communion. In this regard the practice has been consistent with the traditional theology of baptism and communion—the one is prerequisite to the other. Yet the question has to be faced: Should these children within the family of the church be considered as nonbelievers? Is their relationship to the church the same as people who do not participate in its life in any way? Or do these children of church families share some part of the Christian faith? Does their regular attendance and implicit faith make them in some way latent members of the church? If so, what is the relationship between that partial Christian identity and the church's sacraments of baptism and the Lord's Supper? Some Disciples now answer these questions by saying that even before baptism children are members of the covenant and should have the privilege of coming to the Lord's Table as early in childhood as they can "remember Jesus." Other Disciples, however, continue the older tradition of opening communion only to the baptized.

Since midway through the twentieth century, the practice has become increasingly common among Disciples for the children, soon after birth, to be welcomed by the congregation with a service of thanksgiving and blessing. This act of greeting, however, is not clearly understood, and its form and use vary widely across the church. The status of these little ones and their relationship to baptism and the Lord's Supper need to be resolved.

Another factor that is involved in the transformation of baptismal practices is the relationship between membership in the church and citizenship in the civil society. In the earliest days of the church's life, the two memberships were clearly distinct from one another. After Constantine made peace between the church and the empire, the distinction between membership in public life and in religious life began to wither. For a long time the two memberships were virtually identical. Thus it became increasingly easy to justify the baptism of children soon after birth so that their membership in the heavenly realm would be practically equivalent to their membership in the earthly realm. During much of this period of time churches performed certain civil functions including the keeping of records on vital statistics. Parish clergy functioned in part as civil servants. It could be argued that the heart of the culture was Christian, which meant that this confusion of two memberships was a problem only in theory. In practice the two realms worked together so closely that it was hard to distinguish between them.

We live in a time, however, when in most societies of the West the heart of the culture has ceased to be Christian. An ever sharper distinction exists between the principles of the gospel and the principles that rule in public life. Therefore what is increasingly at stake in the topic of Christian initiation is the identification of the Christian life and the determination of what it means to be a Christian. Thus the practice of baptism has to be reconsidered. How can baptism become once again the sacrament of entry into the church's life and be separated from entry into the civil society?

Here too the question is important to Disciples. One of Alexander Campbell's primary interests was the disestablishment of religion. He saw clearly the dangers that were present when the newly born were routinely baptized into the established church of the realm. Infant baptism, he declared, "has carnalized and secularized the church more than any other innovation since the first defection in Christianity.[3] Even though the expectation was that adult baptism would provide for a sharp distinction between church membership and civil affiliation, later history of Disciples and Baptists has not confirmed that expectation. In some parts of the United States, churches practicing believers' baptism are closely identified with the economic, political, and cultural establishment of the community.

Another factor leading to this transformation of baptism has been prompted by concerns over the form of baptism. It is true that characteristically ritual is highly stylized, symbolic, and pruned of many aspects of normal behavior. The physical actions are to express meanings and to convey feelings; rather than accomplish ordinary personal needs such as bathing. In many churches, however, the physical action of applying water in baptism has become so abridged as to mean virtually nothing in experience. Furthermore in many churches the practice of baptism had become so isolated from the worshiping community and so identified with the family itself, that it was hard to see baptism as the initiation into the Christian life and church. The more people think about the ritual action, the more they realize the inadequacies of what has been done.

Even Disciples, despite our practice of baptism by immersion, fall short in the way we conduct the service. The common pattern is for baptism to be preceded by the confession of faith. Persons come forward during a service of worship; in response to questions from the pastor they affirm that they believe in Jesus as the Christ, the Son of the living God. At a later time they are baptized. During the baptism itself, the only words spoken are the baptismal formula itself: "I baptize you in the name of the Father and of the Son and of the Holy Spirit" (Matthew 28:19). While the candidates and the pastor are preparing for the baptism, a worship leader ordinarily speaks to the congregation. A scripture reading about the meaning of baptism may be read and a hymn sung. The congregation benefits from this additional liturgy, brief as it is, but the people being baptized do not because they are out of the room dressing for the rite of immersion. Thus, the reform of the baptismal ceremony is important for Disciples as for other churches.

Another factor that has pushed toward reform of baptism is the renewing of ecumenical relationships. So long as church bodies lived within themselves and minimized contact with other churches, it was possible to maintain their own practices. The more frequent and the deeper the contacts with people in other churches, however, the more necessary it is to become aware of one another's ways of worship and to note similarities and contrasts. The most significant aspect of this ecumenical collaboration has been the impact upon new baptismal liturgies. Although the language continues to vary from one church family to another, the theological content and liturgical forms are remarkably similar.

Because of this ecumenical contact, several churches are giving attention to the Rite for Christian Initiation of Adults (RCIA), developed by the Roman Catholic Church. This new form of the baptismal liturgy is written for what used to be called missionary situations, when the decision to become a Christian required the separation from one way of life and the entering into another one. What is becoming clear to many people in North American churches is that we too are living in a missionary situation. We too are surrounded by people who have had little contact with the Christian faith and way of life. When they come to a church seeking the truth and peace of God, they need to be introduced into a whole new way of life. The RCIA provides the stimulus for all of the churches, Protestant and Catholic, to reconsider their ways of celebrating baptism.

Disciples have been influenced by these ecumenical relationships as have other churches. We too are influenced by other churches' liturgies as we develop our revised ways of doing things. We are being influenced in another, more profound, way too. Our practices of receiving people from other churches by transfer of membership must now be reconsidered. When we Disciples lived in isolation from other church traditions, we were willing to rebaptize people who previously had been baptized as infants or by pouring or sprinkling. We often were unwilling to call this practice rebaptism. Instead, we used phrases like "completing one's obedience to the Lord." The more closely we worship and work with people of other churches, however, the more difficult it is to rebaptize no matter what we have called the practice. Other churches state that the readiness to immerse people already baptized in another way calls into question God's action in the earlier ceremony. Furthermore, they say, when a church rebaptizes people who have already become practicing Christians, it impugns their earlier Christian life and questions the churchly identity of the church in which the earlier baptism occurred. Thus Disciples face the need to consider anew the whole question of what does it mean to baptize.

Indeed Disciples and all of the churches must ask themselves a different question from the one we have most frequently asked in the past. It used to be that when we read theological writings and examined liturgical texts we would ask if they conformed to our own ideas and practices. Now we are encouraged to ask if doctrinal and liturgical writings express the faith of the apostles and the tradition of Christ's church. The criteria for decisions in the church ought not be confined to the previous convictions and practices of one small part of the Christian community. Rather the criteria ought to include the great tradition that began with the apostolic witnesses to Christ and then became the unified witness of the church in its early, developing years.

Characteristics of the New Work Being Done

The result of this period of reevaluation and reformation has been a burst of activity with respect to baptism and related liturgical practice. Four kinds of work should be noted. The first is that the churches have been engaged in drafting new baptismal liturgies that are marked by these qualities:

- They express classical baptismal theology.
- They unite into one action all of the traditional parts of initiation, the pre-baptismal promises, baptism itself, the reception of the Spirit, reception into the Christian community, and admission to the celebration of the Lord's Supper.
- These services of baptism are understood to be fully initiatory.
- They are to be done in the midst of the congregation at worship.
- They recommend that water be used in generous amounts.

A second characteristic of this new period is that very young baptized children are welcomed to the communion table. In principle, children are understood to be communicants from the time of their baptism. No longer is it theologically necessary for them to wait until pre-adolescent understandings of the Christian faith before they can come to the table. As a matter of pastoral practice, some churches still resist admitting children to communion from their early years; nevertheless the trend is clearly in the direction of early communion for baptized children. The time will come when it is rare for baptized children to be prohibited from sharing in the family meal of the Christian community.

A third feature in this period of development is that services of affirmation of baptismal vows and renewal of commitment to Christ are becoming common. Although baptism in its full form includes the confession of faith by the one baptized and participation in a rite in which the newly baptized is touched and a prayer for the Holy Spirit is offered, these two actions can be split off from baptism itself. The new books now propose forms for doing so. One occasion that will be common in all churches that continue to baptize infants is the affirmation of baptismal vows. This service provides an opportunity for people to confess their faith in Christ and thus claim the baptism that took place when they were too young to remember. Although they are not rebaptized, their personal confession of faith takes place in a baptismal setting. After this renewal of their vows, they will participate in a service of laying on of hands and prayer. The combination of these two elements closely resembles the traditional service called confirmation.

It now is being recognized that there are other occasions when people are interested in renewing their baptismal vows. Certain times of transformation in life and experience are so great that it is as though one were beginning over again. Because the churches believe that one should be baptized only once, then something else has to occur. The resolution has been to conduct services in a baptismal context when people can renew again their faithfulness to Christ and receive prayer for the indwelling of the Spirit.

A fourth feature is the development of services of thanksgiving for the birth and adoption of children. These services include expressions of gratitude for the newly received child and pledges of faithfulness in the task of rearing this little one in the Christian faith. These same themes are present in the service of baptism administered to children soon after birth. Yet there are pastoral circumstances in all of the churches that call for a service that is in no way to be understood as baptism. For some, this service takes place early in the infant's life with infant baptism to follow soon thereafter. In many other instances, baptism will be delayed for some time and this service of thanksgiving provides an initial acknowledgment within the church's life that the child is now a part of their care and keeping. These services are closely bound to the natural experience of rejoicing and commitment that are present when a child is born.

The major theological and liturgical work has now been done for the transformation of baptismal practices. Books have been published that present the findings and recommendations of many study teams and editorial groups. The time now has come for the pastors and churches to appropriate the results of this period of reassessment and transformation. The services that follow provide ways for this next step to take place.

A Book of Services

This book presents a collection of services and instructions for study, adaptation, and use. Several of these orders of worship are taken from published sources because these published texts are well conceived and potentially of great value. They have been published in several places and are difficult to bring together in a form that is convenient for use by churches and pastors. The intention in this book is to present these services in one place so that they may become more useful in the liturgical life of congregations.

Some of the baptismal rites and texts have been written for this book. They are intended to provide forms for use in circumstances that have not been provided for in previously published services. These services are supplemented with other materials that are closely related to baptism, including the renewal of vows and activities at the time of birth. Some of these supplemental materials are drawn from the practice of the Christian Church (Disciples of Christ). These Disciples items have been edited and revised in order to bring them closer to the contemporary consensus among the churches. Other items come from other church traditions. These materials have been edited for Disciples use.

The book includes adaptations of two traditional patterns of preparation for Christian baptism. The Easter Vigil is an ancient way of celebrating the Saturday night that leads into Easter morning. This service comes as the climax of the preparation of people who are readying themselves for baptism. There is a recitation of significant events in the history of salvation. Then at the conclusion of the service people are baptized, buried with Christ in death by baptism. Then comes the first celebration of the Lord's Supper for Easter day. In this way the new converts are given the experience of rising with Christ to new life.

This book also includes an adaptation of the Rite of Christian Initiation of Adults. This way of preparing people for baptism combines intense instruction and nurture with brief acts of worship with the congregation on Sunday mornings. It provides a way of evangelism that takes place in worship. The culmination of this approach to instruction in the faith is participation in the Easter Vigil.

The final section of the book contains a group of essays that discuss important issues related to baptism and belonging. One deals with the relation of baptism to Easter. Another discusses children in relation to baptism and the Lord's Supper. The third essay discusses questions related to the baptismal formula.

It takes more than the reform of worship to lead to the renewal of the life of congregations. Yet the serious focusing upon the central affirmations of the gospel is a necessary part of the process of renewal. When pastors and congregations devote themselves to the serious study and use of liturgies of baptism and the renewal of life, they are taking a major step toward the recovery of the power of the gospel and the Holy Spirit in the life of the church.

PART ONE

Baptism

THE DISCIPLES VISION
OF CHRISTIAN BAPTISM

Two vignettes bespeak the variety and unity of baptismal practice among Disciples of Christ. Vignette One: Fourscore Disciples
meet beside a sparkling mountain river on a Sunday afternoon in high
summer. Many in the gathering are children, and they chatter excit-
edly among themselves and to six adolescents who are distinctively
dressed in plain white shirts or blouses and in dark trousers or skirts.
They, along with an adult woman similarly dressed, are candidates
for Christian baptism. The congregation becomes focused as two
elders assist their pastor into the bracing water where the river bends
around a promontory of tall forest pines and ancient gray stone. As
the pastor wades hip-deep against the gentle current, a woman
animates the accordion strapped around her shoulder. The river bank
comes alive with the strains of the hymn, "O Happy Day which fixed
my choice on Thee, my Savior and my God..., Happy Day, Happy
Day! When Jesus washed my sins away!"

One by one the candidates awkwardly and gingerly move out to
their pastor, who turns each one to the proper place beside him.
Offering his right arm to the over-and-under grip of the first young
man, the pastor raises his left hand palm-open in blessing above his
head and intones, "Upon your profession of faith in our Lord Jesus
Christ, I baptize you, my brother, in the name of the Father and of the
Son and of the Holy Spirit. Amen." The pastor's hand of benediction
moves to the middle of the candidate's back for support as he
immerses him backwards against the prevailing current. An instant
later, the new Christian surges up from beneath the water, shining
and new born. Alto and soprano voices raise the strain afresh as each
newly baptized Christian moves back up the river bank into the
warm, dry embrace of deacons with enormous terrycloth bath sheets.
A simple folding table awaits them, set with freshly poured grape
juice and a loaf of home-baked bread. The service concludes with the
Lord's Supper, set for the newest members of this Christian Church

(Disciples of Christ) under the dome of a mountain summer sky.

Vignette Two: The setting is a vaulted sanctuary of graceful dark arches and multi-hued lancet windows. The attention of the two hundred thirty Disciples is fixed upon the elevated baptistry in which the congregation's pastor stands up to her waist in tempered water. Bright flood lights illuminate the winding river scene painted with such care on the back wall of the chamber. Easter lilies festoon the sanctuary, and all the choir is robed in resurrection white. Fifteen youth await their baptismal moments as the pastor carries out a liturgy of the blessing of the water, invoking images of Noah and the ark, Israel at the parting of the sea, and the gracious presence of Jesus at the Jordan River. The pipe organ swells with classic melody as the first candidate meets her pastor in the water and is positioned so that her family can see clearly their daughter's act of faith. The girl offers her handkerchief to the pastor and grips her strong, steady arm. Firmly and clearly, the pastor's voice announces the baptismal formula in the context of full Easter worship, "I baptize you, my sister, in the name of the Father and the Son and the Holy Spirit, One God and Mother of us all." As the youth is plunged beneath the surface of the water, silent prayers rise from the congregation, and children stare up in wide-eyed wonder. Quickly, the newly baptized Christian wades up out of the baptistry and is ushered by deacons into a dressing room where she and her peers towel dry and don fresh clothes for the time of their first communion. Together with the great Easter congregation, they and their loved ones celebrate their initiation into the full membership of the Church of Jesus Christ.

Further examination of actual instances of baptism among the Disciples of Christ would reveal a striking theological unity undergirding every particular variation found regionally or congregationally. Even more notable than this consensus itself is its intuitive character. There is no commonly recognized worship book to regularize baptismal matters for us. Like a family of many branches, the Christian Church (Disciples of Christ) has passed along our traditions in accordance with New Testament understanding and witness, and we have always felt free to innovate so long as the main themes of our tradition remained intact and recognizable. One might say that our steps have been kept by grace from straying from mainstream Christian orthodoxy in baptismal matters, and still, the steps by which we Disciples walk remain our own.

We have been saved from significant errors by our intuitive grasp of the center of true baptismal theology: Through the signs of water and word, God is reaching out to humanity to join us to God's own self. It is this transcendent aspect of Christian baptism that has taught us a truth we did not initiate, and that bids us into covenant partnership with God-in-Christ through baptism. In the preamble to our *Design*, we affirm along with the whole church in every time and place that baptism is ours only as a gift. Though other traditions have much to teach about the language and ritual of baptism, no existing liturgy can exhaust the theological depth and breadth of God's action for humanity in baptism. In accordance with the New Testament, Disciples believe baptism to be in the three-fold name of God and into the body of Christ at large, a catholicity of vision that dates back to the inaugurating documents of our movement.

This conviction that baptism is into the universal church, nothing less than the body of Christ, has helped us turn aside two serious errors. Throughout most of our history Disciples have rejected the idea that baptism is a sectarian rite of induction into a particular religious body. In such a view, the church is little more than an association of like-minded believers who choose to assemble. Baptism becomes a "church ordinance" subordinated to a largely private psycho-spiritual experience of sorrow for sins and catharsis, which leaves the sacramental nature of Christian baptism aside entirely. No linkage is made between baptism and remission of sin, or between the personality of the believer and the sacrament.

Though Disciples have been susceptible to a type of volitional mistake that we shall explore later in the section on rebaptism, we have stood firmly in favor of the sacramental nature of baptism and the high organic doctrine of the church that such baptismal theology represents. The unity of the church is real, personal, and organic, a gift of unity that is present and God-given, and implicit in every instance of true Christian baptism. When Disciples of Christ affirm baptism into the body of Christ rather than into a local or denominational body, we affirm God's initiative by the Holy Spirit, forgiving us our sin and joining us to the whole church ecumenical. Our recent embrace of terms once held suspect among us, like *sacrament*, is one small witness to the wholeness and unity of the church of which baptism is the ritual cornerstone.

Even while speaking of baptism as a rite that accomplishes what it portrays—which is what the word *sacrament* implies—Disciples have resisted a second error. We have been unwilling to accept the idea that baptism, when properly administered, automatically accomplishes its work of forgiveness and new birth. Such a view freezes baptism into a sterile form that demands legalistic adherence and limits the freedom of God. While Disciples have historically affirmed the integral relation between water baptism by immersion and remission of sin, the charge that we practice a "water gospel" is virtually untrue. We continue robustly to practice immersion baptism as the full symbol of the death, burial, and resurrection of Jesus Christ, while repenting for the immersionist legalism of our past. No responsible Disciple would contend these days that God measures out salvation in cups full of water, and our very practice of open communion has militated against such an attitude. God saves us, not we ourselves, even through the exact performance of sacramental word and deed.

The breadth of our sacramental vision and our instinctive scriptural conservatism in matters of baptismal practice have proved attractive to theologians outside our own communion. This appreciation has been voiced in the bilateral conversations proceeding between the Disciples of Christ, and the Roman Catholic and Russian Orthodox Churches. Our immersionist tradition, our identification of adult baptism as the norm for Christians, our emphasis upon the importance of having a clear memory of our own baptism, and our refusal to divide the component of water baptism from the reception of the Holy Spirit by the believer have been noted with appreciation by such persons as Karl Barth, preeminent Swiss theologian earlier this century; and more recently, the German theologian of hope, Jürgen Moltmann, Geoffrey Wainwright, the British Methodist and major contributor to *Baptism, Eucharist, and Ministry*, and William Willimon, whose columns in the *Christian Century* are read throughout the English speaking world.

At the core of Disciples baptismal theology is a profound reverence for the integrity of each person's will and choice. Sadly, some have attributed this respect to ideas generated during the eighteenth century Enlightenment, and mediated to us by our forebears via Scottish common sense philosophy and the rationalism of John Locke. While the Enlightenment did make ideas like the value of the individual available to the wider culture, it did irreparable damage to the sort of liberty wrought by the grace of God in Christ by transmuting it into "the inalienable rights of man," and cutting these "rights" off from their theological roots. "Rights" and "grace" have remote relations at best, and our Disciples forebears clearly preferred the apostle Paul to John Locke in baptismal matters.

When God calls human beings to be reconciled through baptism, it is one at a time, a fact recognized by Disciples of Christ. Baptism is the more intimately personal of the two sacraments. We believe that the integrity of our decisions to become obedient to God in baptism is vouchsafed to us not as reprieved criminals but as God's dear children by the death, burial, and resurrection of Jesus Christ who is Lord and Savior of each as well as all. The center of gravity for baptism, the sacrament of justification, is always located in God's gracious initiative to reach out to us. Nevertheless, perhaps all the more, the outreach of God to us each in baptism, so personal in nature, calls for a deep response of our wills. This response may never be private and still be called Christian, but it must never be less than personal in order to be proper to Christian baptism as we Disciples understand it.

This invitation to respond personally to God's call to gospel liberty in Jesus Christ fired the second great awakening on the American frontier in the early nineteenth century. So compelling was this call that Disciples founder, Barton Warren Stone, baptized men and women at the Cane Ridge revival until he "spat blood" from the exertion; and our greatest evangelist, Walter Scott, the author of the famous "five-finger exercise," baptized more than ten thousand during his career in the Western Reserve.

When this deeply personal call to Christian discipleship has centered itself in the praise and honor of God, it has issued in a profound witness to God's new social order on earth as in heaven. Following the best of our Anabaptist heritage, Disciples have understood obedience to God in baptism as the first ethical action of human life. As Menno Simons, the persecuted Anabaptist bishop of the sixteenth century, taught, baptism is the least of God's commandments, and whoever would be faithful in the weightier matters of nonviolence, love of neighbor as we love ourselves, and allegiance to God before any human state or institution, must first be faithful to the call of the apostle, "Repent and be baptized." In this sense, baptism is the root of all Christian ethical action, the indelible sign that our lives and fortunes belong to God and not to us. We Disciples are rooted in the ethics of the resurrected Christ by virtue of our baptisms. We affirm that though there may have been good choices in our lives chronologically earlier than our response to God's grace in baptism, our baptismal obedience to Christ is basic to all our ethical actions wherever and whenever we are true to our baptismal vows.

The political ramifications of Christian baptism in this key are likewise profound. Alexander Campbell, a self-exile from strife-torn Northern Ireland, understood that an alliance between the coercive power of the state and the spiritual power of professional churchmen meant the co-opting of the gospel into a state ideology, a civil religion. A religion whose membership roll is virtually identical to the tax rolls of the state too easily "makes a pact with the devil" in Campbell's view, and his struggle against pedo-baptist moralists and ideologists in the Sunday Mails dispute, and against the Moral Societies that sprang up largely in Presbyterian congregations, confirmed him in this view.

The church was not ever to be confused with the state according to Campbell, and baptism was the Jordan flood that separated the two. Infant baptism traditions embraced the Constantinian wedding between rule by divine right and Christendom. The dream of a Christian nation became a nightmare for dissenters from the religious majority, and Campbell affirmed the true political content of so-called believers' baptism when he announced that there was no Christian nation on the face of the earth other than all those in every land who are baptized into Christ and who by their confession and manners evidence their obedience to him in all things. To be baptized into Christ as Disciples practice it, then, may at its best be a blow against tyranny and a strong witness that Christian diversity is not the accident of history but the very intention of God.

Disciples have understood baptism as the prime ordination to Christian ministry. No theological bar exists to any baptized believers who are designated by their congregation to baptize, administer the Lord's Supper, preach, teach, or any of the other functions usually considered the prerogative of the ordained ministry of other traditions. Any other ordination to Christian ministry is secondary to Christian baptism. Following the divine imperative given to the apostle Peter, that what God has cleansed, we are not to call common, Disciples have honored the work of the Holy Spirit in the life of the baptized believer, and have opened ourselves to the priesthood of all believers in a thorough-going way. Our understanding of baptism has led us to this high opinion of the laity, yet in such a way as not to denigrate the clergy.

This emphasis upon the role of the human will in baptism can lead to error or confusion. For example, what is to be said about the baptism of infants or others not able to speak for themselves? Is it baptism, as most churches claim, or is it not? And how are such people to be received into the church? By "rebaptism," or by transfer? The ecumenical discussions Disciples are carrying on with other churches, and our own commitment to the full enfranchisement of all Christians around the Lord's Table, have brought the advisability of rebaptism into serious question, and have called a great number of our congregations and the whole Christian Church (Disciples of Christ) beyond the local congregation to renounce the practice. For the foreseeable future, a minority of our congregations will continue closed membership practices, but the issue is joined among us and the tide is clearly with open membership and the renunciation of rebaptism.

The volitional mistake that is at the bottom of this problem manifests itself in a variety of ways. Some believe that they "didn't know what baptism was" when they were baptized, and new knowledge or understanding has made rebaptism necessary. Others have undergone crises in life that they believe have rendered their previous lives and commitments null and void. Some come to us from infant baptism churches and request immersion after having become convinced that it is the fuller form, and one they feel incomplete as Christians without undergoing for themselves. Still others yearn for a deeper spiritual commitment to Christ and his church, and they can think of no more significant way to make it than by a new baptism.

The virtues of each of these impulses for rebaptism are debatable, especially since Disciples in the main understand baptism as unrepeatable. Pastorally, however, there is a measure of spiritual renewal evident in each of them. The question that properly confronts a church that is renouncing rebaptism is how to respond constructively and positively to sincere Christians who are seeking to develop themselves spiritually.

Needless to say, we Disciples must face our volitional error at its base and root, and repentantly correct it. Any insinuation of human will into the role of arbiter of our salvation must be exposed and refuted. No individual is sovereign, no matter how valuable to Christ he or she is. Only God saves, and without the death, burial, and resurrection of Jesus Christ, "all our fighting would be losing," as Martin Luther confessed. Disciples must reassert the initiative of God in every aspect of our baptismal theology in order to redress the false exaltation of human will or experience or knowledge as prerequisite to a valid baptism. Our wills respond to God's call to us in Christ to repent and be baptized, to invite us to belong to the family of God in the church. Never do we initiate.

Yet the aspect of baptism that includes response to the gospel call is essential if the benefits of baptism in ethics, politics, and ministry that we have discussed are to be realized "on earth as in heaven." The striving of the Holy Spirit within us to deepen our commitment is surely akin to the yearning of the Holy Spirit the apostle Paul perceived in all creation for the full reconciliation and renewal he called "adoption as children of God."

Disciples' evangelical tradition offers a way to satisfy this valid need of many for a public and ritual renewal of their baptisms. We commonly offer an opportunity for people to respond to the gospel call during each service of worship. Called "the invitation to Christian discipleship," this moment of worship gives leave to those who wish to come to the front of the sanctuary and make their dedications to God. Normally, this time is appropriate for confessions of faith and commitments to become obedient to Christ in baptism. Many Disciples clergy use this invitation to call for those who are already Christians to make rededications of their faith.

In essence, this practice is none other than a renewal of the vows we have made at our baptisms. Individual Disciples come to answer "yes" when asked to reaffirm their faith in Jesus Christ as Son of the living God. Properly administered by the pastor, this personal rededication serves as an extension of baptismal vows and an affirmation of baptismal memory, rather than as their negation. Follow-up through pastoral care and education, and through a congregational emphasis upon spiritual growth, prayer, eucharistic life, Christian social responsibility, and renewal, can and will deepen the sacrament of baptism in the lives of believers. Thus, the impulse toward revival of faith is seized upon and developed, while rebaptism is rendered unnecessary as well as theologically wrong.

Disciples of Christ are a covenantal people joined to God and each other in the love of God in Jesus Christ. Baptism is the great gift of sacramental reconciliation that initiates us into Christ and through him into the whole people of God. It is the least of God's commandments, the needle's eye through which the faithful pass to newness of life. By the signs of humble water and human words, the divine purpose is affirmed, and the ordinary way of yielding ourselves to the service of God is made manifest. Disciples of Christ have imperfectly understood and performed it, but it is Christ, after all, who is the Lord of baptism. We have never attempted to usurp his prerogative to use our church to glorify God and to serve the people. To these ends we have made a baptismal theology that is diverse, practical, and personal. Where we have intuitively made the right decisions, may Christ be praised. Where we have erred, may Christ have mercy and aid us in the amendment of our baptismal understandings.

Over the years Disciples have developed a pattern for celebrating baptism. Although there are slight variations from congregation to congregation, the main elements are consistently found; the invitation to Christian discipleship, the confession of faith, baptism.

The invitation to discipleship expresses a central truth of the Christian faith: God calls; women and men respond. At an earlier time in our history the invitation was focused upon the call to confess faith in Christ and be baptized. In time, other appeals (as described earlier in this essay) were added—the call to transfer membership and for public rededication of life. Understood in the light of the primacy of God's call, the invitation is sacramental. The invitation is a means of God's grace, a ritual formula of words and deeds that gives witness to the quickening of faith in the believer. While we and our formulations of the invitation are integral and not incidental to God's will and purpose, the response of women and men to our appeals is empowered by none other than the Holy Spirit. Thus, we are always led to confess at every fruitful invitation we proffer, "This was the Lord's doing and it is wonderful to see" (Matthew 21:42b, *Jerusalem Bible*).

Disciples of Christ characteristically offer the invitation immediately following the sermon, as a way of responding to God's call through preaching. The hymn of invitation usually is integral to Disciples' practice, and care should be exercised in its selection. Who gives the invitation is a matter of congregational choice, but the preacher for the day is most effective and appropriate. The invitation must be heard clearly; but if some form of amplification is used, a traveling microphone is far better than speaking from behind the pulpit. The inviter should be at floor level with the congregation when the call to Christian discipleship is given. There should be no steps or other obstacles between the inviter and those who are being invited to respond.

Baptism, the immersion of the one who has confessed faith, often takes place in a service subsequent to the one when the confession occurred. Whenever possible, Christian baptism should be carried out during the regular service of worship on the Lord's Day. The sermon for the morning may serve as an invaluable instruction to those about to be baptized, and they should be present in the sanctuary to hear their pastor open the riches of the scriptures to them on the matter. By robing for baptism prior to the beginning of the service, the candidates for baptism may be seated with the congregation during the service of the Word. Following the blessing of the water, the candidates are escorted by deacons to the entrance to the baptistry.

Suggested themes and texts for the preacher on a baptismal Sunday are: baptism as a cleansing bath (see Ephesians 5:26; Hebrews 10:22; 1 Corinthians 6:11; Titus 3:5), a new birth (see John 3:5; Titus 3:5; 1 Peter 1:3; 2:2), a gift of enlightenment or illumination (see Ephesians 5:14; Hebrews 6:4; 10:32), "burial" with Christ (see Colossians 2:12), "resurrection" with and in Christ to newness of life (see Romans 6:4–5; 8:11; 2 Corinthians 5:17; Ephesians 2:15), and incorporation into the body of Christ, now animated by the Holy Spirit (see 1 Corinthians 12:13; Ephesians 4:4–6). The accounts of the baptism of Jesus (see

Matthew 3:13–17; Mark 1:9–11; Luke 3:21–22; John 1:29–34), and of others (see Acts 2:37–42 for the 3000 on the day of Pentecost; 8:12–17 for the Samaritans; 8:26–40 for the Ethiopian; 9:1–19 for Saul/Paul; and 10:44–48 for the first pagans) give opportunity to call the congregation to remember their own baptisms. Types of baptism in the Hebrew scriptures, the exodus through the Red Sea (see Exodus 14:15–31), the crossing of the Jordan River (see Joshua 3:7—4:18), and Noah and the ark (Genesis 6:13—8:22; 1 Peter 3:21) are available and useful, as are texts that deal with baptism with water and the Holy Spirit (see Acts 1:5; 2 Corinthians 1:21–22), and with baptism and the triune God (see Matthew 28:18–20).

Rites and Texts

A. THE INVITATION

OPENING SENTENCES FROM THE BIBLE

The pastor shall say:
The apostle Peter said to the people on the Day of Pentecost, "You must repent, and every one of you must be baptised in the name of Jesus Christ for the forgiveness of your sins, and you will receive the gift of the Holy Spirit" (Acts 2:38, *Jerusalem Bible*);

or

Jesus said, "Come to me, all you that are weary and are carrying heavy burdens, and I will give you rest. Take my yoke upon you, and learn from me; for I am gentle and humble in heart, and you will find rest for your souls. For my yoke is easy, and my burden is light" (Matthew 11:28–30);

or

"What is good has been explained to you.…This is what Yahweh asks of you: only this, to act justly, to love tenderly and to walk humbly with your God" (Micah 6:8, *Jerusalem Bible*).

THE CALL

The pastor issues the call to Christian discipleship. Included in the call will be the invitation (1) to confess faith in Jesus Christ and for acceptance into candidacy for Christian baptism; (2) to join the congregation by transfer from another congregation; and (3) to reaffirm one's baptismal vows by public rededication of faith. Each of these opportunities for response to God should be clearly stated at each invitation.

The pastor shall say words to this effect:
God is calling some of you to claim the promise that was made to generations past, the promise that is now, by the power of the Holy Spirit, offered to you. That promise is new life in Jesus Christ. Today we appeal to all who desire this new life to confess your faith in Jesus who died that we may live. As scripture says, "If your lips confess that Jesus is Lord and if you believe in your heart that God raised him from the dead, then you will be saved. By believing from the heart you are made righteous; by confessing with your lips you are saved" (Romans 10:9–10, *Jerusalem Bible*). God calls you now to express this faith by being baptized

into Christ. In baptism you are buried with him and emerge to live
a new life (see Romans 6:3–11; Galatians 2:16–20; Colossians 2:12;
2 Corinthians 5:17; and Ephesians 2:15).

God is calling others of you to join the full life of this congregation
by coming forward to transfer your church membership. You
have already confessed Christ and been baptized. Your place in
the family of God awaits you here, with sincere love and hospi-
tality (see Romans 12:13; and Hebrews 13:1–2).

God is calling still others of you to reaffirm your Christian faith in a
public way by rededicating yourself to Christian discipleship. For, as
God has spoken, "I live in a high and holy place, but I am also with
the contrite and humbled spirit, to give the humbled spirit new life,
to revive contrite hearts" (Isaiah 57:15, *Jerusalem Bible*).

On God's behalf, we appeal to you to respond to God, as the
congregation stands and sings the hymn of invitation.

B. Confession of Faith

*Upon determining that a respondent has come forward to confess faith in
Jesus Christ, the pastor calls the name of the person out clearly to the
congregation and says:*
  Name comes before God and this congregation today to confess
  Jesus Christ as Lord and Savior.

Turning toward the respondent, the pastor says:
  Name, do you, with Christians of every time and place, confess
  that Jesus is the Christ, the Son of the living God (Matthew 16:16,
  RSV)? Do you further commit yourself to live a life pleasing to
  God, and to remain faithful to your confession so long as you shall
  live? If these are your intentions, you shall answer, "I do."

*The pastor offers the new believer a sign of acceptance and Christian
affection, such as a handshake or embrace, and says:*
  On behalf of this congregation, I receive you as a candidate for
  Christian baptism, and I rejoice with you in your faith and trust
  in God. May God who has called you to this commitment grant
  you the courage to keep your vows and grow in grace. Amen!

C. Rededication of Faith or Renewal of Baptismal Vows

*Upon determining that a respondent has come forward to renew a commit-
ment to the Christian life, the pastor declares the name of the person and the
person's desires to the congregation. Then the pastor says:*

Name, you come before God and this congregation today as a baptized believer in Jesus Christ, and a member of the body of Christ. Do you reaffirm and renew the vows first made at your baptism? Do you reaffirm that Jesus is the Christ, the Son of the living God, and renew your trust in his lordship and his saving work? Do you further rededicate yourself to a life pleasing to God and declare your intent to remain true to your confession as long as you live? If these are your intentions, you shall answer, "I do."

As at a confession of faith, the pastor greets the respondent with affection and says:

May God, who has called you to renew your vows, grant you the grace to keep true to your commitment and grow in grace. Amen!

D. TRANSFER OF MEMBERSHIP FROM ANOTHER CONGREGATION

If the respondent(s) comes forward to join the congregation by transfer of membership, the pastor announces the name(s) of the respondent(s), and, when appropriate, the congregation(s) from which they come. Then the pastor says:

Name, you come before God and this congregation today to join us in serving God and the whole creation in love and justice. To seal this decision, I ask you to reaffirm the faith you confessed at your baptism. Do you believe that Jesus is the Christ, the Son of the living God, and do you accept him as your Lord and Savior, as he is the Lord and Savior of the world? Further, do you declare your recommitment to a life pleasing to God and to God's purpose in the world, so long as you live? If these are your intentions, you shall answer, "I do."

Then, greeting the new transfers with warmth and affection, the pastor says:

On behalf of the spirit of the risen Christ and this congregation, I welcome you to a new life of witness and service among us. May God, who has called you to this decision, grant you courage to keep true to your vows and to grow in grace. Amen!

The congregation may say:

With joy and thanksgiving, we welcome you into Christ's church; for we are all one in Christ. We promise to love, encourage, and support you, to share the good news of the gospel with you, and to help you know and follow Christ.[4]

The pastor normally concludes the service with a prayer to God to send the Holy Spirit upon each person as is appropriate to the commitment each has made. Also the prayer invokes the Spirit upon the whole congregation as they receive these newly committed persons into their worship and witness.

It is also appropriate at this time to lead the congregation into an affirmation of their faith, such as the Preamble to the Design for the Christian Church (Disciples of Christ), or some other affirmation, such as the Apostles' or Nicene Creeds, or the Affirmation of Faith of the United Church of Christ. The pastor may also wish to call upon the congregation to conclude this segment of worship with a verse from a hymn, such as, "Blest Be the Tie That Binds," or "Now Thank We All Our God."

E. BAPTISM[5]

OPENING SENTENCES

Standing near the baptistry, or in the water, the pastor or other worship leader leads the congregation in sentences of worship and a reading from the Bible.
God be with you.

Response: **And also with you.**

Sisters and brothers, there is one body, and one Spirit, just as you were summoned into one and the same hope when you were called.

Response: **There is one Lord, one faith, one baptism, one God and Father of all (Ephesians 4:5–6).**

THE READING OF THE BIBLE: Romans 6:3–11

THE BLESSING OF THE WATERS

Standing in the water, the pastor says:
Lift up your hearts.

Response: **We lift them up to God.**

Let us pray.

Holding a vessel of water, the pastor says:

We praise you and thank you, O God.
You have led us to the water of life.

Before the world was made, you breathed upon the face of the
deep.
You made dry land appear.

You bless the earth with life-giving rain.
You make the wasteland bloom.
You are the Lord of the storm and the flood.
You speak and they are still.
Send now your Holy Spirit upon this water,
that it may become your servant in the mystery of baptism.

(The pastor pours a generous stream into the baptistry.)

You cleanse us with the waters of forgiveness.
You wash away our sins.
From the rock you make living water spring.
You quench the thirst of your people.
Send now your Holy Spirit upon this water,
that it may bathe your children clean of sin and death,
and satisfy all who thirst for your righteousness.

(The pastor pours a second generous stream into the baptistry.)

We praise you, O God, for your Son, Jesus Christ.

He is the Lord of the waves.
He speaks and they subside.
By the waters of regeneration he cleanses our iniquities.
He gives us new life.
He is the rock from whom living waters flow.
He died for us because he loved us.
But you raised him from death and revealed him as Lord and
Savior of the world.
Teach us to die with him that we may share in the fullness
of his life.
Baptize us in the living water of his Spirit
and unite us and all women and men in his peace. Amen.

(The pastor pours the rest of the water into the baptistry.)

THE IMMERSION

*One by one the candidates enter the baptistry and are positioned by the pastor
who then asks:*

Name, do you turn from your sin and renounce all manner of evil and
injustice? Do you turn to Christ Jesus as your Lord and Savior?

The candidate says: I do.

Name, upon your confession of faith in Jesus Christ, I baptize you in the name of the Father and of the Son and of the Holy Spirit. Amen.

or

Name, upon your confession of faith in Jesus Christ, you are now baptized into the name of the Father and of the Son and of the Holy Spirit. Amen.

The candidate is immersed. Then, immediately after the baptized has recovered stable footing, the pastor places his or her hands on the head of the new Christian and says:

Dying, Christ destroyed your death;
Rising, Christ restored your life.
Receive the gift of the Holy Spirit!

The newly baptized Christian is led out of the baptistry.

THE CONCLUSION

Let us give thanks to the Lord our God.

Response: **It is right to give God thanks and praise.**

Let us pray:

The pastor then prays for the growth in faith of the newly baptized Christians.

An appropriate hymn concludes the service of baptism and allows the pastor and the newly baptized Christians to meet in the sanctuary for the Lord's Supper, which is the culmination of the day's worship. Before the benediction, the pastor gives each new Christian the handshake or embrace of fellowship, and welcomes each one into the membership of the church. In the event that the newly baptized have sponsors and/or family members present, they are all invited to stand with the pastor at the exit (if space permits), and the congregation is encouraged to welcome them and congratulate them personally.

ECUMENICAL SERVICES
OF BAPTISM

This section of *Baptism and Belonging* presents two comprehensive orders of baptism. Each of these orders illustrates the theology and form of new baptismal rites that have been published by the churches acting separately and by ecumenical bodies. Baptismal services published since 1970 are quite varied in their detail and arrangement of parts. In general, they are divided into three segments: the service of the Word, the baptismal covenant, and reception into the church.

These orders for baptism are to take place during the public worship of the congregation, especially in services on Sunday. It is assumed that baptism is preceded by a clear proclamation of the Word of God in the context of praise and confession, and that baptism is followed by the celebration of the Lord's Supper. Indeed, the order for baptism appropriately takes the place of other forms of the service of the Word. Recently published services suggest scripture readings, although it is understood that on Sundays the lectionary texts for that day could take precedence. By featuring baptism several Sundays of the year, pastors develop the major themes of baptism over a period of time. Thus a congregation is able to have its knowledge of the first sacrament expanded and deepened over the course of years.

In addition to readings and sermon, this first segment of the rite of baptism includes the presentation of persons to be baptized. Sponsors present the candidates to the pastor. Candidates and their sponsors are asked if the candidates want to be baptized. Services will include promises by those soon to be baptized, in which they reject the other loyalties that have bound their lives in the past; and they commit themselves to a new loyalty to Jesus Christ.

This first portion of the baptismal liturgy ordinarily includes prayers for the people who are to be baptized. It is understood that the action soon to take place will make great demands upon them as they seek to live the Christian life. Thus it is only right that God be praised for their readiness to confess Christ and that God be asked to strengthen

31

them with the Holy Spirit for the new life that they are to receive.

In some traditions, such as the Disciples of Christ, these special aspects of the service of the Word have been part of the more private conversation between pastor and people soon to be baptized. One of the great values of the new liturgies is that a portion of this instruction is moved from the privacy of pastoral counseling into the public life of the church. These promises and prayers deserve to be made in the presence of the whole people of God so that everyone knows and everyone shares in the petitions that God be present in this baptism and the life that follows it.

The second division in the services of baptism can be called the baptismal covenant. Here are concentrated the central elements of this sacrament of forgiveness and new life. The baptismal covenant begins with the confession of faith in Jesus Christ. Through the generations, the church has phrased this confession in different ways. Initially, when the converts were already deeply imbued with the Jewish faith in God, the new development was their faith in Jesus Christ. Thus the earliest confessions in scripture focus upon this affirmation that Jesus is the Messiah. The confession of Peter in Matthew 16:16 is an example of this sharply focused confession of faith. Today in many congregations these words of Peter continue to be the central affirmation of faith that leads to baptism.

After it was no longer possible to assume that converts knew about the Jewish faith, a fuller statement of loyalty and belief became normal practice. Converts were taught to believe in the one God, self-revealed in three persons. Certain other doctrinal convictions were also compressed into this central statement of apostolic teaching, which took on the name "The Apostles' Creed." Historical records make it clear that the normal custom was for converts, either by themselves or in concert with the worshiping congregation, to confess this faith as the beginning of their baptism.

Even today the dominant practice throughout most of the church is for baptism to occur in the context shaped by the recitation of this brief statement of Christian belief in God and trust in Christ. In this way the solidarity of the church in all times and places is manifested. New Christians are linked with the faith of the apostles and the witness of the martyrs. They are embraced by the faith that has sustained the church and inspired its theologians. These ancient words, despite their archaic form, continue to speak today. Many Disciples now find that when they speak this testimony to the apostolic faith, their sense of identity with the church universal is strengthened.

A second part of the baptismal covenant, now much more evident than had been true in earlier liturgies, is a long prayer over the water. Just as the bread and communion wine are blessed prior to their reception by the congregation, so the water of baptism is blessed in preparation for its use in Christian baptism. The prayers vary in their detail but are remarkably similar in their form. They begin by giving thankful praise to God for the ways in which God has worked through water from creation until now. The chief focus, however, is upon this water that will now be used in the sacrament of baptism. The prayer is that God will use this water as the means whereby the divine act of forgiveness and regeneration occurs.

Then comes the baptism itself, which is the washing of the candidates in this holy bath. Over the generations there has been much debate concerning the amount of water and how it is applied. The new services all agree that water should be used in abundance and the recommendation that immersion be the form is widespread. We do not know how early Christians baptized, although it is clear from biblical records that they went down into the water. It may be that they stood or knelt in a shallow pool and then large quantities of water were poured over them three times, in the name of the Father and of the Son and of the Holy Spirit. In later times water was used more sparingly, and in the churches today the majority practice continues to be the sparing use of water. Yet baptistries for the immersion of adults are being built in churches that previously had not conducted baptism this way. The trend is clearly in this direction and is one in which many people rejoice.

As the person is baptized, the pastor doing the baptizing speaks the formula that declares God's work and implicitly asks God to do it now. While the New Testament was still being formed this formula adopted the trinitarian form: "I baptize you (or, you are baptized) in the name of the Father and of the Son and of the Holy Spirit." Ever since then, baptisms have been performed in this name. Christian identity is defined by this God whose oneness is expressed in three persons. People everywhere can thereby claim that they are members together in the one church for we have all been baptized in "the strong name of the Trinity" (to quote from an ancient Irish hymn). Many people are striving to find other ways of naming the God who is self-revealed as "three in one and one in three." One of the most common is "Creator, Redeemer, and Sustainer." Another, which rearranges the traditional order, is "Wisdom, Love, Might." These formulations stress the things that God does and distinguishes the persons of the Godhead by function. In contrast, the classic formula of Father, Son, and Holy Spirit stresses the personhood of God and distinguishes the persons on the basis of their relationship to one another. Until this theological debate about God's name is resolved, it is important that the classic formula be used. What is at stake is our identity as Christians and our full membership in Christ's body the church. (A fuller essay on this topic is printed in the final section of this book.)

The baptismal covenant includes one more element, a prayer for the Holy Spirit. Some traditions have assumed that the indwelling presence of the Holy Spirit comes automatically with baptism and needs no other liturgical expression. Today the tendency is strong for services of baptism to include an explicit prayer for the Holy Spirit. This prayer is often accompanied by dramatic acts such as laying on of hands or marking the forehead of the one baptized with the sign of the cross and blessed oil. In some of the liturgies this prayer for the Holy Spirit occurs immediately after the baptism itself, so close to the baptismal action that it is hard to separate the two. In other liturgies there is a slight delay so that the prayer for the Spirit comes as a new phase to the complex baptismal liturgy.

The third segment of the baptismal liturgies can be called welcome and reception into the church. In some of the services it begins with illustrative symbolism. People are given gifts such as a white robe or a candle as signs of their new life in Christ. The liturgies will usually include some form of welcome whereby the church as a whole or its chosen leaders receive the newly baptized into the life of the congregation and denomination of the baptizing church.

The high point of welcome, however, is the receiving of the Lord's Supper. In this second sacrament the church's life of faith and source of strength are both realized. Thus whatever may have been the previous relationship of the newly baptized to communion, a new dimension now has emerged. They are full participants in the life of the church and thus are fully able to enter into the family meal of the congregation.

Rite One. This service, published in 1973, was developed by a committee representing the churches in the Consultation on Church Union, along with representatives from Roman Catholic and Lutheran churches. There was full participation by Disciples during the process of developing this service and commentary. The intention was not to develop a "common denominator" approach to baptism, meaning a service that concentrated on what all of the participating churches could traditionally agree on. This kind of approach always focuses on the past and what has previously prevailed among the participating churches. Rather the intention was to express the consensus that was emerging in the participating churches and more broadly in the

Christian world. This approach, while committed to a strong historical perspective, also projected forward the developments that the
committee believed were going to shape the common life of churches
in years to come.

Four qualities characterize this order for baptism. First, it is
informed by classical baptismal theology with its themes of forgiveness of sins, incorporation into Christ, reception of the Holy Spirit,
and entrance into the heavenly community. This service assumes that
baptism is the commissioning of people for the ministry of service in
the life of the world. Second, Holy Baptism is a rite for adults, with
provisions for the incorporation of small children. In this way the
COCU service departs from a point of view that infant baptism is the
norm and adult baptism is the variation.

Third, this service is presented as a complete service of initiation,
thus uniting parts that often are separated in pastoral practice in the
churches. It begins with the service of the Word, continues with
prayers, and then concentrates upon the confession of faith and
baptism. Following baptism, come the prayer for the Holy Spirit and
welcome into the church. The service concludes with the celebration
of the Lord's Supper. While the commentary assumes that there will
be occasions when the service is divided into constituent parts and
done on different occasions, the operating assumption is that initiation is a unified event in its meaning, regardless of how divided it may
be in its administration.

Fourth, this service provides for full participation by the congregation. Perhaps the most important focus for the congregation is
when the people of the church join with candidates and their sponsors
in confessing the Christian faith.

Rite Two. This liturgy was developed by Disciples on the Commission on Theology sponsored by the Council on Christian Unity. It
is more complete than traditional Disciples baptismal services have
been. It surrounds the confession of faith, still derived from Matthew
16, with other promises by the one being baptized and by the
congregation. There is a prayer of thanksgiving and intercession
offered over the water that is to be used for baptism. The welcome into
the Christian community is explicitly stated.

Despite the strength of this order for baptism, when it was first
published it did not include an explicit calling upon the Spirit to
descend upon the one baptized. As revised for this book, it offers a
text and procedure for adding this traditional element.

These two services could be used by Disciples in different circumstances. The first is that the full baptismal service become the service

of the Word on Sunday morning, taking the place of the way that the congregation ordinarily does the first part of the service. The second way that these comprehensive rites could be used is when a service of baptism is planned in its own right. On some occasions, such as Pentecost afternoon, a congregation may decide that there will be a service that revolves completely around baptism and initiation into the Christian life. In such a service, it would be important that the liturgy be full, complete, and richly suggestive in its theological and pastoral contents.

Rites and Texts

RITE ONE[6]

The celebration of baptism begins with a liturgy of the Word, including the reading of one or more passages of scripture, a sermon, and a prayer. Baptism is followed by a general prayer of intercession and the ministration of the Lord's Supper, beginning with the offertory.

In emergencies the rite of baptism may be abbreviated, but must always include the administration of water in the name of the Father, the Son, and the Holy Spirit.

For the liturgy of the Word one or more of the following passages may be used.

Genesis 12:1–4a	*Galatians 3:27–29*
Genesis 17:1–8	*Ephesians 4:1–7*
Deuteronomy 6:1–7	*Hebrews 12:18–25*
Exodus 14:26—15:2	*Titus 3:4–7*
Isaiah 63:15–16	*Matthew 28:16–20*
Ezekiel 36:24–28	*Mark 1:1–11*
Acts 2:36–42	*Mark 10:13–16*
Romans 6:1–11	*John 3:1–8, 16*

Following the liturgy of the Word candidates for baptism, with their sponsors,[7] are presented to the congregation. Where appropriate, parents shall accompany candidates at their presentation and may serve as sponsors. The pastor says:

> These persons have come to the family of Christ seeking (*for themselves and their children*) his gifts of peace and power: peace with God and all his creatures; power to live life that is joyful, free, and devoted to the good work for which God has made us.

The pastor then addresses the candidates (and sponsors):

> Before laying down his life for his friends, our Lord Jesus Christ gathered his followers together to tell them of the life to which he calls all people:
>
> > "If any want to become my followers, let them deny themselves and take up their cross and follow me. For those who want to save their life will lose it, and those who lose their life for my sake, and for the sake of the gospel, will save it" (Mark 8:34–35).

Jesus promised that God would send them the power of his Holy
Spirit so that they might be able to live a new life, following his
own example of suffering love and joyful obedience to God. On
Pentecost that promise was fulfilled. By God's Spirit the waiting
band of disciples was made new. With glad and generous hearts
they praised God and found favor with all the people.

Is it now your desire that *you/this child* be baptized
into death with Christ who breaks the power of sin?

The candidates (or the sponsors) say:

That is my desire.

Is it your desire that *you/this child* be raised to
new life with Christ, sharing in his work of reconciling love?

That is my desire.

Is it your desire that *you/this child* be joined to the
people of God and its ministries of service in the name of Jesus
Christ?

That is my desire.

The pastor may address the sponsors:

As sponsors (*parents*) you have presented *this/these* candidate(s)
for Christian baptism.

Will you nurture *him/her/them* in the Christian faith that *he/she/
they* may respond to God's grace, confess the Christian faith, and
lead the Christian life?

We will.

The pastor may address the congregation, now standing:

As the body of Christ in this place, will you continue to care for
these candidates and help them, in every way possible, to grow
to maturity in Christ?

We will.

The candidates for baptism (with their sponsors) and the pastor
go to the baptistry. While necessary preparations are being made,
there may be hymns and psalms, other scripture lessons, silence,
and prayers for the candidates.

When all are ready, the pastor may offer this or an alternate prayer:

We thank you, God, for water. By it you give life to plants and animals and all persons. By this gift you nourish us with life's necessities and you offer us cleansing and refreshment.

Through the waters of the Red Sea you led your people Israel out of slavery into the inheritance of a new land. To the waters of the River Jordan our Lord Jesus came to be baptized. Today we praise you because by water you enfold us in the death of Christ and from the water you raise us, in resurrection like his, into the power and peace of those who believe in him.

Calling upon your name, O God, we come to this water. By the power of your Holy Spirit, make it a cleansing flood that washes away sin and gives new life to these who today confess the name of Christ. Bind them into the Christian community of love, joy, and peace, destroying the hostilities that divide. As you did on Pentecost, baptize them in your Holy Spirit that they may be strong to do your work of reconciling love until that day when you make all things new.

To you, Holy God, be praise and honor and worship through your Son Jesus Christ with the Holy Spirit, one God for ever and ever. Amen.

At the baptism the pastor asks each candidate (or sponsors) to declare the Christian faith, using either form 1 or form 2 below. Or, the candidates (or sponsors) may speak in unison, using either of the forms. Or the candidates (or sponsors) may use form 1 after which the congregation joins them in a unison recitation of form 2.

FORM 1

Do you believe in the one God, creator of all things?

I believe.

And in Jesus Christ, God's only begotten one, redeemer of the world?

I believe.

And in God the Holy Spirit, who unites the church in love?

I believe.

FORM 2

I believe in God, the Father almighty,
creator of heaven and earth.

I believe in Jesus Christ, God's only Son, our Lord,
who was conceived by the Holy Spirit,
born of the Virgin Mary,
suffered under Pontius Pilate,
was crucified, died, and was buried;
he descended to the dead.
On the third day he rose again;
he ascended into heaven,
he is seated at the right hand of the Father,
and he will come to judge the living and the dead.

I believe in the Holy Spirit,
the holy catholic church,
the communion of saints,
the forgiveness of sins,
the resurrection of the body,
and the life everlasting. Amen.

The pastor may address the candidate (or sponsors) *saying:*

What is your *(this child's)* name?

The pastor shall immerse each candidate in water, or pour water on the candidate's head, saying:

Name, I baptize you in the name of the Father and of the Son and of the Holy Spirit. Amen.

or

Name, you are baptized in the name of the Father and of the Son and of the Holy Spirit. Amen.

The pastor may place a hand on the head of each person, making on the forehead the sign of the cross (using oil prepared for this purpose, if desired),[8] and say:

You are sealed by the Holy Spirit and marked with the sign of Christ's cross, that you may know him and the power of his resurrection and the fellowship of his sufferings.

When all have been baptized, the congregation (or one of the elders or the pastor) says to them:

The life you now live, live by faith in the Son of God who loved you and gave himself for you. The grace of the Lord Jesus Christ, the love of God, and the fellowship of the Holy Spirit be with you.

or

Once you were strangers and sojourners; now you are fellow citizens with us in the household of God. Rejoice. The grace of the Lord Jesus Christ, the love of God, and the fellowship of the Holy Spirit be with you.

Then the pastor and other members of the congregation greet the newly-baptized and each other with words and gestures of love and peace; and they may say:

The Peace of the Lord be always with you.

And also with you.

The service continues with the intercessions, including prayers for the newly baptized and their sponsors, after which follows the ministration of the Lord's Supper. The newly-baptized may be welcomed to the Lord's Table at this time; or, if it is in keeping with the practice of the church, they may be welcomed to the Lord's Table upon their subsequent affirmation of Christian faith.

RITE TWO[9]

DECLARATION OF THE MEANING OF BAPTISM

Pastor or Elder:

Baptism is the sign of new life through Jesus Christ. Through baptism, we are brought into union with Christ and with his church around the world and across the ages. Through baptism, we participate in Christ's own death and resurrection. Through baptism we assume a new identity, committing ourselves to a life of love and righteousness.

As we approach this profound moment in the life of the church and of this [these] individual(s), let us remember the many dimensions of baptism revealed to us in scripture:

> "Do you not know that all of us who have been baptized into Christ Jesus were baptized into his death? Therefore we have been buried with him by baptism into death, so that, just as Christ was raised from the dead by the glory of the Father, so we too might walk in newness of life."
>
> Romans 6:3–4

> "As many of you as were baptized into Christ have clothed yourselves with Christ. There is no longer Jew or Greek, there is no longer slave or free, there is no longer male and female; for all of you are one in Christ Jesus."
>
> Galatians 3:27–28

> "Peter said to them, 'Repent, and be baptized every one of you in the name of Jesus Christ so that your sins may be forgiven; and you will receive the gift of the Holy Spirit. For the promise is for you, for your children, and for all who are far away, everyone whom the Lord our God calls to him.'"
>
> Acts 2:38–39

> Finally, we recall how Jesus himself, baptized by John in the waters of the Jordan, commanded his followers to "make disciples of all nations, baptizing them in the name of the Father and of the Son and of the Holy Spirit."
>
> Matthew 28:19

RENUNCIATION OF EVIL AND PROFESSION OF FAITH

The pastor invites the candidate(s) and their sponsors to come forward.

Name, the community gathered here welcomes you with great joy to this holy celebration! Baptism is both God's gift and our human response to that gift. We pray for the transforming presence of God's Spirit and we ask that you respond to God's grace by repenting of your sins, by renouncing evil, by affirming your faith, and by committing yourself(selves) to grow in a life of Christian discipleship.

Do you repent of sin and earnestly pray for God's healing forgiveness?

I do.

Do you renounce being ruled by the false gods of this world—the snare of pride, the love of money, the power of violence?

I do [renounce them].

Do you, with Christians of every time and place, confess that Jesus is "the Christ, the Son of the living God"? (Matthew 16:16).

I do [so believe].

Will you strive, with God's help, to follow Christ through faithful witness and loving service as part of his body, the church, all the days of your life [lives]?

I will [so strive].

Addressing the congregation, the pastor asks:

Will you, the community here gathered, continue to uphold *Name* with your prayers and your witness in remembrance of your own baptism?

We will.

The pastor may ask the congregation to confess the Christian Faith using the Apostle's Creed:

I believe in God, the Father almighty,
creator of heaven and earth.

I believe in Jesus Christ, God's only Son, our Lord,
who was conceived by the Holy Spirit,

born of the Virgin Mary,
suffered under Pontius Pilate,
was crucified, died, and was buried;
he descended to the dead.
On the third day he rose again;
he ascended into heaven,
he is seated at the right hand of the Father,
and he will come to judge the living and the dead.

I believe in the Holy Spirit,
the holy catholic church,
the communion of saints,
the forgiveness of sins,
the resurrection of the body,
and the life everlasting. Amen.

BAPTISMAL PRAYER

Gracious God, we thank you that in every age
you have made water a sign of your presence.
In the beginning your Spirit brooded over the waters
and they became the source of all creation.
You led your people Israel
through the waters of the Red Sea
to their new land of freedom and hope.
In the waters of the Jordan,
your Son was baptized by John
and anointed with your Spirit
for his ministry of reconciliation.
May this same Spirit
bless the water we use today,
that it may be a fountain
of deliverance and new creation.
Wash away the sins of those who enter it.
Embrace them in the arms of your church.
Pour out your Spirit on them
that they may be pastors of reconciling love.
Make them one with Christ,
buried and raised in the power of his resurrection,
in whose name we pray.
Amen.

BAPTISM

The celebrant leads each candidate into the baptistry and lowers him or her backward into the water after saying the following words:

By the authority of Jesus Christ, I baptize you, *Name,*
in the name of the Father and of the Son and of the Holy Spirit.
Amen.

or

Name, by the authority of Jesus Christ, you are baptized in the
name of the Father and of the Son and of the Holy Spirit. Amen.

Immediately after the administration of the water, as hands are placed on the head of each person by the pastor and by others if desired, the pastor says to each:[10]

The Holy Spirit work within you,
that being born through water and the Spirit
you may be a faithful disciple of Jesus Christ.
Amen.

or

The Holy Spirit be upon you, *Name,*
child of God,
disciple of Christ,
member of the church.

WELCOME

Other prayers for the baptized and the welcome may come immediately after the baptism or at the time of the Lord's Supper, at which the newly baptized should be especially served.

A prayer for the baptized may be said, using one of the following or the pastor's own words.[11]

Pastor: We give you thanks, O Holy One,
           mother and father of all the faithful,
           for *this your child/these your children*
           and for the grace acknowledged here today
           in water and the Holy Spirit.
           Embrace us all as sons and daughters
           in the one household of your love.
           Grant us grace to receive, nurture, and befriend
           this new member/these new members

of the body of Christ.
Amen.

People: **Give to the newly baptized:**
strength for life's journey,
courage in time of suffering,
the joy of faith,
the freedom of love,
and the hope of new life;
through Jesus Christ who makes us one.
Amen.

or

Pastor: Merciful God, you call us by name
and promise to each of us your constant love.
Watch over *Names.*
Deepen *their* understanding of the gospel,
strengthen *their* commitment to follow the way of Christ,
and keep *them* in the faith and communion of your church.
Increase *their* compassion for others,
send *them* into the world in witness to your love,
and bring *them* to the fullness of your peace and glory,
through Jesus Christ our Lord.
Amen.

The pastor and congregation may welcome the baptized using this responsive declaration:

Pastor: *Name,* God has blessed you with the Spirit
and received you by baptism into the one,
holy, catholic, and apostolic church.

People: **We welcome you into the bonds of Christian fellowship!**
Together, with Christians of all races and nations,
we are members of Christ's body,
united by Christ's blood into one family of faith.

Pastor: Through baptism you have put on Christ,
passing from darkness into light.

People: **May you grow in the knowledge and love of God.**
May your faith shine as a light to the world.

Commentary

Baptism, as the sacrament through which one is formally incorporated into the church, should be administered, whenever possible, during public worship (including the celebration of the Lord's Supper). This enables the members of the congregation to welcome the newly baptized person(s) into the body of Christ, to be reminded of their own baptismal vows, and to pledge themselves to be a community of continuing nurture.

The baptismal liturgy may come either 1) between the opening prayers and the proclamation of the Word through the reading of scripture and preaching, or 2) between the sermon and the celebration of the Lord's Supper. The latter is theologically more appropriate, signifying that baptism is a response to the Word of God and an entry into the eucharistic community. The former has the practical advantage of allowing the newly-baptized persons more time to dress before returning to the congregation to participate in the Lord's Supper.

The normal Disciples practice of assigning baptism to the pastor of the congregation is to be encouraged since such persons are set apart for representative, sacramental leadership and they symbolize the universal connectedness of Christ's church. Other members of the church, and especially the elders, may, with the consent of the congregation baptize.

The words of the service are said by the celebrating pastor unless otherwise noted. The first three sections of the baptismal service should take place near the congregation—perhaps on the steps of the chancel—in order to underscore the participation and support of the worshiping community. Following the baptismal prayer, the congregation may sing a hymn or hymns as the celebrant and candidate(s) prepare for the actual baptism. It would be appropriate for the candidate(s) to be already robed, a sign of "putting on" a new life in Christ, during the first part of the liturgy. This would also make for a quicker transition to the baptistry. Otherwise, the candidate(s) will need to robe during the hymn.

The opening lines of the "declaration" are drawn from the World Council of Churches' theological convergence document, *Baptism, Eucharist and Ministry* (BEM), paragraphs 2, 3, and 6 in the baptism section, and from the Consultation on Church Union's *COCU Consensus*, Chapter 6, paragraph 10. The major breakthrough represented by BEM may be the willingness of churches to acknowledge that the biblical witness regarding the meaning of baptism is richer than their separated traditions have taught. The passages used above lift up multiple images or meanings that yet point to a single reality.

Acts 2:38 and 2:39 have been used polemically by advocates of, respectively, believers' and infant baptism. They should be read together as a corrective to such polemics.

The practice of sponsors,[12] unfamiliar to most Disciples, has much to commend it. These persons commit themselves to a special nurturing responsibility for the baptismal candidate, thus signifying (a) the community's role in the response of faith and (b) the necessity of continual growth in faith after baptism.

The scriptural paragraphs in the Declaration of the Meaning of Baptism remind the candidate(s) and congregation that baptism is both a gift of grace and a response of faith, and prepare them for the questions that follow. The renunciation, focusing on contemporary forms of idolatry, is adapted from Max Thurian, "An Ecumenical Baptismal Liturgy," in *Baptism and Eucharist: Ecumenical Convergence in Celebration.* (Alternative phrasing could be: "Do you turn away from the false gods of this world—loving yourself more than God and neighbor, loving things more than God or each other...?")

The typical form of the Good Confession used in Disciples congregations is "Do you believe that Jesus is the Christ, the Son of the living God, and do you take him as your Lord and Savior?" While such a formulation has the advantage of stating an intimate relationship between Jesus and the believer, the second part of the question has two drawbacks: First, it opens the way for the saving work of Christ to be construed as an individualistic relationship with little regard for the corporate and cosmic dimension of salvation. Second, it is the language of nineteenth-century revivalism and not of scripture. Thus, it is recommended that the candidate(s) repeat Peter's simple confession as it appears in Matthew. Such a profession should be included in the baptismal liturgy in order not to separate the saving initiative of God through the Spirit from our personal appropriation of its benefits through trusting response.

Disciples insist that creeds articulated in the history of the church not be made "tests of fellowship" at the time of baptism. Persons come to this decision of faith, however, within the context of the universal church and of local communities whose faith is more fully developed than the simple confession of Peter. Thus, the candidate(s) might appropriately join with the whole congregation at some other point in the worship service in recitation of a broader confession of faith (especially the Apostles' Creed, a baptismal confession from the early church).

A prayer asking God to bless the water and recalling God's use of water in the history of salvation is standard in Roman Catholic, Lutheran, and Anglican baptismal liturgies and is increasingly common in other churches. One reason for this prayer is that it makes explicit that water is not the effective agent, nor is the faith of the one being baptized. Nor is the power of the church what makes the change. Rather, God who is invoked in this prayer brings about new birth. The strong emphasis in BEM on the activity of the Holy Spirit is, likewise, an affirmation that baptism is not a ritual or human initiation ceremony that we do, but, most fundamentally, an act of God.

There is objection in parts of the church to the masculine imagery of this traditional trinitarian formula (from Matthew 28:19). There are also defenders who see "Father" as an intimate description of our relationship with God, given us by Jesus, and who regard its use in baptism as an expression of continuity with the apostolic church. Other formulas raise other problems: All human language about God is symbolic and must be used carefully. This topic is addressed more fully in one of the essays later in this book (see the essay beginning on page 140).

The welcome described in this section is a focused, public expression of the informal and nonliturgical welcome normally extended by Disciples congregations following the worship service.

Some Disciples congregations are discovering that various symbolic acts, such as the anointing with oil [13] as a sign of the gift of the Spirit or the giving of a candle as a sign of passing from darkness into light, can reinforce the significance of the ceremony as well as give powerful expression to its meaning. Other congregations extend "the right hand of fellowship" as a gesture of welcome into this community of faith.

BAPTISM IN SPECIAL CIRCUMSTANCES

Introduction

Ordinarily the people who come to be baptized in Disciples congregations are able on their own behalf to confess faith in Jesus Christ and be baptized by immersion. Some come or are presented for baptism, however, whose physical or mental condition makes it difficult or impossible for them to confess the Christian faith or be immersed in the ordinary manner. How should congregations, elders, and pastors respond? In these special circumstances, how do we Disciples, as a community of believers, express and ritualize the good news of Jesus Christ with theological integrity and pastoral sensitivity?

Theological integrity is important. Central to the practice of baptism is the proclamation of the good news of God who is made known to us in Jesus Christ. This faith in God and hope for salvation are offered through baptism, proclaimed by baptism, and received in baptism. People who are ready to confess the Christian faith and request baptism ordinarily make these desires known in a service of worship. There they make their confession of Jesus Christ. Ordinarily, they are baptized in this same context and there received into the life of the church.

Pastoral sensitivity is also important, for circumstances arise in which these ordinary conditions are in some way modified. Among them are these:

Someone who is infirm or critically ill makes the confession of faith in Jesus Christ, but immersion is either impractical or impossible. Usually such a person cannot be present for a regular worship service of the congregation.

The parents of an infant who is critically ill or stillborn ask that their child be baptized.

Someone who is confined to a wheelchair or in some other way physically restricted confesses Christ and is ready to be baptized. Yet immersion is difficult.

Someone who is confined to a facility cannot come to the church building to confess faith or be baptized.

Historically, Disciples have understood baptism to be an act that is done for the remission of sin. Baptism is, in the opinion of Alexander Campbell, an act in which only "penitent believers...not infants nor adults, but professors of repentance toward God and faith in Jesus Christ, are proper subjects."[14] This view excludes from baptism persons who cannot make a confession of faith or a profession of repentance, or be immersed, especially in the context of worship.

Disciples, however, believe that God, not the church, is the author of salvation and adds to the church those whom God chooses. Therefore, the baptism of persons whose circumstances can be described as special or unusual provides an opportunity for a congregation to enlarge its understanding of God's grace and expand its understanding of baptism beyond the normal practice of public confession and immersion.

Disciples also believe that God uses the preaching of the Word and the administration of the sacraments as the normal means of approaching people. This confidence is the foundation for worship, for preaching, for baptizing, and for remembering Christ at the communion table. The church does what it does because it believes that God wants it to act this way and blesses its actions by using them to accomplish the divine will. Yet we also believe that God's power and love transcend all such sacramental speech and action. God can and does work in every human situation with the possibility that faith and new life may come.

The theological and pastoral task, therefore, is to uphold the normal practice of preaching and sacramental action—and at the same time to be open to modifying that practice when it is necessary to do so. The God who uses sacraments to save us can also save us without sacraments and with sacraments adapted to the unusual circumstances encountered in human life.

One of the tasks of the leaders of the church, especially pastors and elders, is to make the adaptations that seem to be necessary. These leaders discern the situation of those coming to baptism and assess the degree of exception therein represented. They too are the ones who, in the light of scripture and the Christian tradition, decide what to do and how to adapt the baptismal rite.

In all of this activity, however, the leaders act not in their own name but in the name of the congregation that they represent. Thus, affirmation by a congregation of the act of baptism and of the person who is baptized is essential when baptism takes place outside the context of a worshiping congregation. Such affirmation helps the newly baptized person maintain connection to a congregation. The act of affirmation also helps the congregation maintain connection to the person who has been baptized, especially if the person is unable to attend church. Through an act of affirmation, the baptized person is welcomed by the congregation into the community of faith. Affirmation by the congregation may incidentally provide an opportunity for the congregation to create rituals of welcome for persons whose acceptance of Christ has led them to be baptized.

Theologically, the most difficult adaptations for Disciples are those in which the candidates are not able to speak for themselves. Their mental capacities may be such that they cannot grasp the preaching of the gospel. They may be injured or gravely ill and thus not able to speak or signal their response. Indeed, there may be some question as to their capacity to hear, let alone to respond in faith. The one brought to baptism may be an infant who is critically ill, or who may have been stillborn. All of these circumstances challenge the theological claim that baptism presupposes the conscious faith decision of the one being baptized.

One pastoral response to such circumstances is not to baptize, but to offer a service of blessing and intercession. In such a service the church embraces the person who cannot speak, whatever the reason, and affirms God's love for the person. Then the church intercedes with God that the divine love will accept this one and enter the person's name into the book of life. The anointing with oil with prayer can be part of this pastoral action.

Yet in these circumstances baptism is also one of the ways that the church has responded. This practice is based on the following convictions. First, the primary actor in baptism is neither the candidate nor the church but God. Second, even though much of the language of baptism is declarative, the underlying intention is petitionary. When the church baptizes, it declares God's offer of new life and it prays that God will grant this new life to the one now buried with Christ in a death like his.

But what of the method of baptism? As immersionists, how do Disciples understand baptism by another method of baptism (pouring, sprinkling, a water-drenched hand placed on the candidate's forehead)? Most Disciples will agree that immersion is the normative and most appropriate form of Christian baptism.[15] Many Disciples will further agree that baptism by immersion ought not be viewed as "the only or exclusive form of Christian baptism." God blesses other modes of baptism with the new life in the Holy Spirit. How can Disciples, even though we are confident of the efficacy of immersion of penitent believers in normal circumstances, insist upon baptism in that same mode when those circumstances are not present?

In addition to the theological rationale for baptism in unusual circumstances, there is a pastoral dimension. Baptism is a strong witness to the church's care of parents who are faced with the unspeakable agony of watching their child die. It offers grace and comfort to a person who makes a confession of faith while in a sick bed. Baptism adapted to special circumstances assures people in wheelchairs or confined in other ways that they are cared for by God and by the church. Baptism adapted to special circumstances offers pardon to one who believes that his or her circumstance is the result of an offense against God. It offers calm and courage to persons who are confronted by their own fears of death.[16]

Whenever special circumstances require the adaptation of the rite of baptism, one principle should be observed: The words and actions ordinarily used for baptism are the basis for baptisms under special circumstances. The pastor, elders, and other leaders of the service are to make whatever adaptations in language and action are required by the circumstances themselves. Yet even adapted services need to include the central features of the rite of Christian baptism.

The full service of baptism is outlined below, with notes and explanations that may apply in special circumstances. The following section contains illustrative texts for baptism and related rites for use in several circumstances. They may be used in the place of other texts that appear elsewhere in this book or used as guides to modify the language that ordinarily would be used.

The Service in Outline

Preparation

If the person(s) to be baptized cannot be present with the congregation for baptism in a regular service, then baptism may be celebrated in the hospital, home, or other location. Normally the pastor will be accompanied by members of the family and one or more elders of the congregation. When it is pastorally appropriate, other members of the congregation and friends may also be present.

Sponsors from the family or congregation may be present with the one to be baptized. When those being baptized cannot speak on their own behalf, sponsors speak for them.

The preparation includes the following elements adapted to the specific circumstances:

Statement concerning baptism into Christ
Reading(s) from the Bible
Comment or application of the biblical teaching

Claiming the Christian Faith

Claiming the Christian faith includes the following elements adapted to the specific circumstances. The service always includes the confession of faith in the triune God.

Renunciation of evil
Affirmation of the new life in Christ
The confession of faith
Prayer for the candidates

The Baptism

The candidates are baptized with water, in the name of the triune God. Special arrangements or procedures may be needed in order to take the candidate into the water for immersion. If immersion is not possible, water is poured on the forehead or applied in some other manner that the candidate can feel.

The baptism includes the following items:

Thanksgiving over the water
The baptism
The blessing (and anointing)

The Welcome
> An elder or other Christian welcomes the newly baptized. When appropriate, a brief order of the Lord's Supper follows.

Rites and Texts

A. FOR SOMEONE CRITICALLY ILL

STATEMENT

> Through baptism we are joined to Christ
> in death and resurrection
> and enter into the covenant
> that God has established.
> In this covenant, the grace of God
> sustains and strengthens our faith
> with the gift of life eternal
> which is ours in Christ.
> Jesus Christ, our risen Savior,
> is our comfort and hope.
> Christ brings us to wholeness of life
> in this world and in the world to come.

RENUNCIATION AND AFFIRMATION

The renunciation of evil may include words such as these:

> Do you turn away from the passions and powers
> that have held you captive?

> **I do.**

> Do you turn toward God
> seeking forgiveness and the restoration of life?

> **I do.**

PRAYER FOR THE CANDIDATE[17]

> Be present, O Lord, to your servant *Name*
> with your heavenly grace,
> that *she/he* may continue yours forever
> and daily increase in your Holy Spirit more and more,
> until *he/she* comes to your everlasting kingdom.
> Amen.

Eternal and loving God,
we come in thanksgiving to the baptism
of your servant *Name*.

We pray your continued blessings upon *him/her*
that at this hour and in time to come
he/she may trust in your presence and power.
Amen.

Most gracious God,
you have promised your grace and forgiveness
to those who earnestly seek you.
We pray that you will extend
to your servant *Name* a full measure
of your grace and forgiveness in this life,
at the hour of death, and
in eternal life to come.
Amen.

THE WELCOME

Name, by your baptism you have become
a living member of Christ's body, the church.
In the name of your sisters and brothers in Christ
I welcome you and greet you with signs of peace.
May the loving embrace of this community
bring you peace and joy in Jesus Christ.
We pray that day will come soon
when we meet together around Christ's communion table
and there receive his body and blood.
May they be the life-giving substance
that strengthens us in this world
and prepares us for life in the world to come.
Amen.

B. For an Infant in Critical Condition

1. SERVICE OF PRAYER

This service may be used in church, in a hospital, or in the home. It is appropriate for use whether the infant is stillborn or alive.

PSALM

God is our refuge and strength,
a very present help in trouble.

Though my flesh and my heart fail me,
you, O God, are my portion for ever.
Forsake me not, Holy One,
go not far from me, my God.
Hasten to my help, God of my salvation.
Why are you so full of heaviness, my soul,
and why so unquiet within me?
O put your trust in God
whom I will yet praise,
who is my deliverer and my God.[18]

COMMENDATION (AND ANOINTING)

The pastor may anoint the child on the forehead or other suitable part of the body with oil.[19]

Let us commend this child to the love of God.

and

God of compassion,
we have anointed your child *Name*
with this oil of peace.
Caress *him/her*,
shelter *him/her*,
and keep *him/her* in your tender care.
We ask this in the name of Jesus our Savior.[20]
Amen.

or

Gracious God, by your love
you gave us life,
and in your love you have given us
new life in Jesus Christ.
We entrust this child
to your merciful keeping
in the faith of Jesus Christ,
who died and rose again to save us,
and who now lives with you and the Holy Spirit
in glory for ever and ever.
Amen.

PRAYERS

One or more prayers such as the following may be offered.

Gracious God,
in darkness and in light,
in trouble and in joy,
help us to trust your love,
to serve your purpose,
and to praise your name;
through Jesus Christ our Savior.
Amen.

Loving God,
in your mercy you have brought
your daughter *Name*
through childbirth in safety.
May she know your support
in this time of trouble
and enjoy your protection always;
through Jesus Christ our Savior.
Amen.

Almighty God,
you make nothing in vain,
and love all that you have made.
Comfort *Name(s)* in *her/their* sorrow,
and console *her/them* by the knowledge
of your unfailing love;
through Jesus Christ our Savior.
Amen.

2. SERVICE OF BAPTISM

This service may be used if the infant is living.

STATEMENT

Jesus said that we are born anew of water and the Spirit.
That which is born of the flesh is flesh;
and that which is born of the spirit is spirit.
Jesus also said that God does not desire
that anyone perish but that all receive eternal life.
Therefore we bring this little one to be baptized
trusting that God will grant *him/her* life forevermore.

The pastor or elder may say to family and friends:

Do you desire that *Name* be baptized?

Response: **I (we) do.**

PRAYER FOR THE ONE BEING BAPTIZED

God of steadfast love,
from whom we come and to whom we shall return.
With love we bring *Name* to you.
As *she/he* is baptized with water,
baptize *her/him* with your Holy Spirit
that *she/he* may be born into life eternal.
We pray through Jesus Christ
who received the little children into his arms
and blessed them.
Amen.

or

Merciful God, as mothers hold their little ones
in their arms of love and tenderness,
so you enfold us in your steadfast love.
In your tenderness embrace this child
whom we bring to be baptized
by water and in the Holy Spirit
that *she/he* may become a living member
of your everlasting family.
Minister to those who care for *her/him*
that our love may increase in its tenderness
and our trust in you grow stronger.
Amen.

C. For a Wheelchair-Bound Person

STATEMENT

Baptism is the sign of new life in Jesus Christ.
Through baptism we are brought into union
with Christ and with his church
around the world and across the ages.
Through baptism we participate in Christ's
own death and resurrection.
Because death no longer holds dominion over us,
we can yield ourselves—
heart, mind, body, and soul—

as a living sacrifice to God.
Through baptism we assume a new identity,
committing ourselves to a life of love,
righteousness, and faithful service.

RENUNCIATION AND AFFIRMATION

The renunciation and affirmation may include words such as these:[21]

Do you renounce sin and the power of evil
in your life and in the world?

I do.

Do you renounce any thought, word, or action that
would keep you from trusting God
and from living the Christian life?

I do.

Do you renounce the attitudes and habits
that imprison your spirit
and keep you from fullness of life?

I do.

Do you pledge yourself
to be Christ's faithful disciple,
to glorify the name of God,
and to love your neighbor?

I do.

PRAYER FOR THE CANDIDATE

Holy God, you give life to all creation,
and inspire hope in all whom you have made.
Renew in us the eager longing to
become your children.
Bless now your *son/daughter*
that *he/she* may be freed from all that holds in bondage,
and be possessed by the liberty
that belongs to your sons and daughters.
Through Jesus Christ who, at your right hand,
continually intercedes for us.
Amen.

D. For Someone Confined

STATEMENT

Jesus came by the power of the Spirit
to preach good news to the poor,
release to the captives,
recovering of sight to the blind,
liberty for those who are oppressed,
and the acceptable year of God, the Holy One.
Inspired by this gospel of hope we are baptized
into the holy commonwealth of God,
confessing our sins
and yielding ourselves to God
who through Christ has reconciled the world
to God's own self.

RENUNCIATION AND AFFIRMATION[22]

Do you renounce the powers of evil
and desire the freedom of new life in Christ?

I do.

Do you confess Jesus Christ as Lord and Savior?

I do.

Do you promise by the grace of God,
to be Christ's disciple,
to follow in the way of our Savior,
to resist oppression and evil,
and to show love and justice
as best you are able?

I promise, with the help of God.

Do you promise,
according to the grace given you,
to grow in the Christian faith
and to be a faithful member
of the church of Jesus Christ,
celebrating Christ's presence
and furthering Christ's mission
wherever you go?

I promise, with the help of God.

PRAYER FOR THE CANDIDATE

Holy One, wherever we go,
your Spirit searches and finds us.
Whatever we think, you know our thoughts.
By your Holy Spirit come to be with us
in this place where we have gathered.
Especially do we pray for your servant *Name*
who today confesses the name of Christ
and is baptized by water and the spirit.
By your hand lead *him/her* and
by your strong hand hold *him/her* fast.
This we pray through Jesus Christ
who calls us to liberty in the holy commonwealth
that is to come.
Amen.

WELCOME

On behalf of Christ's church
I welcome you into communion with all
who have confessed the name of Christ
and been baptized.
We rejoice in the pilgrimage of faith
that has brought you to this sacrament of hope.
And we pray for that time when
you will be able to join
your Christian brothers and sisters
as they gather to hear the Word of God
and offer their sacrifices
of praise and thanksgiving.

E. CONGREGATIONAL AFFIRMATION OF THE NEWLY BAPTIZED

This service, adapted to specific circumstances, is recommended for use when baptism has taken place in settings other than the worshiping congregation.

The affirmation of the newly baptized should take place in a regular Sunday service of the congregation as soon after baptism as possible.

The affirmation liturgy may take place at the invitation to discipleship or at the prayers of the people.

INTRODUCTION

The pastor announces that the baptism has occurred away from the congregation, names the newly baptized, and invites elders, family, and sponsors who witnessed the baptism to come and be with the pastor during the service of affirmation.

After announcing the baptism, the pastor continues, speaking to the congregation.

> As many of you as were baptized into Christ
> have clothed yourselves with Christ.
> There is no longer Jew or Greek,
> there is no longer slave or free,
> there is no longer male and female;
> for all of you are one in Christ Jesus.
> *Galatians 3:27–28*

> For the promise is for you, for your children
> and for all who are far away,
> everyone whom the Lord our God calls.
> *Acts 2:39*

Do you affirm and celebrate the baptism of *Name*?

We do.

Do you promise to pray for *him/her*,
and to love, support, and care for *him/her*
through the life of this congregation?

We do.

PRAYER OF AFFIRMATION

Holy God, through Jesus Christ
you offer forgiveness and new life
to people in every circumstance.
Today we remember and celebrate the baptism of *Name*.
Bless *him/her* with the power of your Holy Spirit
that *he/she* may grow in faith, in knowledge,
and in the Christian way of life.
May *he/she* become a living member
of Christ's body, the church,

and a faithful witness to the love of Christ,
in whose name we pray.
Amen.

or

God of love, today we remember *Name*
who was baptized by water and the Spirit.
May *he/she* and all who by baptism
have been joined with Christ in a death like his
also share in his resurrection life.
Through our Savior Jesus Christ we pray.
Amen.

THE EASTER VIGIL

The following service is offered as a way for the congregations of the Christian Church (Disciples of Christ) to participate in the larger church's recovery of Easter Vigil. In its celebration of Easter, the ancient church included the baptizing of those who had been preparing for that moment. On Easter eve, those to be baptized and the full community of believers assembled in the darkness to celebrate the coming light of new life in Jesus Christ.

A fuller discussion of Easter Vigil for the Christian Church (Disciples of Christ) is offered in Part Three of this book.

Outline and Description of the Service

The order of worship for Easter Vigil comes to us from early in the third century of the church's history. It has four parts:

A Service of Light
A Service of the Word
A Celebration of Baptism
A Celebration of the Lord's Supper

The Service of Light has three sections: lighting the fire, processing with the paschal candle and proclaiming the resurrection of Christ. The lighting of the fire and candle may be an adoption by the early church of the Jewish home ritual of lighting the lamps on Sabbath eve. During the procession, the paschal candle is raised three times to words affirming, "Christ, our light!" The Easter proclamation is an ancient hymn, "Exsultet," which is used only once a year. In it the church rejoices with the angels over Christ's victory, which brings our salvation.

The Service of the Word recites the history of salvation. It portrays the instruction of the candidates for baptism during early centuries of the church. As many as twelve lessons may be read. Enough readings are to be chosen to portray the broad sweep of salvation. Lessons essential for the service are the creation account (Genesis 1), the exodus narrative (Exodus 14) and the resurrection story from the Gospel of the day. The sermon may be omitted. If a sermon is preached, it is to be very brief. The readings are sufficient to carry the proclamation in this service.

The celebration of baptism is the culminating act to the recital of salvation history that the congregation has just experienced in the Service of the Word. The baptismal liturgy includes the confession of faith by candidates and congregation, blessing over the water, baptism, prayer for the Holy Spirit, and the renewal of baptismal vows of all the faithful. If there are no candidates for baptism, the service comes to focus on the renewal of the vows of baptism.

The Lord's Supper concludes the service of Easter Vigil. The usual rites of the congregation may be used or they may be supplemented with material in the Easter Vigil service offered here.

When is the Vigil to be held? In the early third century, Hippolytus counseled that the service is to go from sundown Saturday to cockcrow Sunday. Because of the elemental power of light and dark in Easter worship, the service ought to begin after darkness falls. It may begin late Saturday and, at midnight, carry over into early Sunday with the celebrative portions of the worship: baptism and the Lord's Supper. Or, at nightfall on Saturday, an abridged service may occur that is oriented toward families. Or, it may start before dawn on Sunday. The worship moves from the contrast of light breaking into dark in the Service of Light, to the Vigil in dim light, to the brightening of full day during baptism and communion. Care needs to be taken in timing the service so that worshipers know in advance how long the service takes. Also, a long Vigil on Sunday morning, followed by breakfast, may crowd the schedule for the mid- and late-morning celebrations of resurrection.

Congregations that observe a prolonged Vigil or Chain of Prayer through Saturday may reverse the Service of the Word and the Service of Light. The readings in the Service of the Word will then serve as a conclusion of the day-long Vigil with the whole assembly keeping the last watch of the Vigil. It is most dramatic if the Service of the Word can be timed to conclude at midnight. The first act of Easter is the Service of Light.

The service offered is an adaptation of the Great Vigil of Easter from the *Book of Worship: United Church of Christ*, (United Church of Christ, Office for Church Life and Leadership). Included in the service are prayers adapted from *The Book of Common Prayer* (Seabury), *Handbook of the Christian Year* (Abingdon), and *Thankful Praise* (CBP Press).

Order for the
Great Vigil of Easter

Service of Light
 Lighting a New Fire
 Greeting
 Blessing of New Fire
 Lighting of the Paschal Candle
 Easter Proclamation

Service of the Word
 Greeting
 Old Testament Readings
 Act of Praise
 New Testament Readings
 Sermon
 Hymn

Service of Water
 Greeting
 Blessing of Water
 Baptismal Vows
 Blessing of the People
 The Baptism
 Prayer for the Baptized
 Hymn

Service of the Bread and Cup
 Offering
 Welcome of the Newly Baptized to the Table
 Greeting of the Newly Baptized and Passing the Peace
 Prayer at the Table
 Receiving Bread and Communion Wine
 Prayer After Communion
 Dismissal
 The Benediction

Rites and Texts

SERVICE OF LIGHT

LIGHTING A NEW FIRE

*The people may assemble in silence outdoors or within the darkened church.
A small fire may be started on the ground or in an urn or pan that will safely
contain it. When the ceremony is held indoors, the people may face the rear
of the sanctuary toward an entrance where the ceremony is held. When the
fire is ready, the leader may proceed with the greeting.*

GREETING

The congregation stands as a leader greets the people in these or other words.

Leader: Grace to you from Jesus Christ,
who was, and is, and is to come.

Sisters and brothers in Christ,
on this most holy night
when our Savior Jesus Christ passed
from death to life,
we gather with all the church
throughout the world in vigil and prayer.

This is the Passover of Jesus Christ:
Through light and the word,
through water and the bread and wine,
we recall Christ's death and resurrection,
we share Christ's triumph over sin and death,
and with invincible hope,
we await Christ's coming again.

Hear the word of God:
In the beginning was the Word,
and the Word was with God,
and the Word was God.
In the Word was life,
and the life was the light of all humanity.
The light shines in the darkness,
and the darkness has not overcome it.

BLESSING OF NEW FIRE

A leader, located near the flame, may offer one of the following or a similar prayer.

Leader: Let us pray.
Eternal God, giver of light and life,
bless this new flame,
that by its radiance and warmth
we may respond to your love and grace,
and be set free from all that separates us
from you and from each other;
through Jesus Christ,
the Sun of Righteousness.
Amen.

or

Eternal Lord of life,
Through your Son you have bestowed
the light of life upon all the world.
Sanctify this new fire and grant
that our hearts and minds also be kindled with holy desire to
shine forth
with the brightness of Christ's rising,
and to feast at the heavenly banquet; through Jesus Christ our
Lord.
Amen.

LIGHTING OF THE PASCHAL CANDLE

A leader, using a taper, may take a flame from the fire and light the paschal candle,[23] *saying these or similar words.*

Leader: May the light of Christ,
rising in glory,
illumine our hearts and minds.

FIRST RAISING OF THE PASCHAL CANDLE

Immediately after the words above, the bearer may raise the paschal candle, and the following words may be said or sung responsively.

Cantor: (or Reader)
Christ our light.

People: **Thanks be to God.**

If individual candles are provided for the congregation, the process of lighting them may begin after the first raising of the paschal candle. The one bearing the paschal candle, and all other leaders, may process toward the table. When the ceremony is held outdoors, the entire congregation may share in the processional into the church. When the ceremony is held indoors, the smaller procession may move from the entrance to the chancel. As the procession moves forward, all candles other than those on the table may also be lighted.

SECOND RAISING OF THE PASCHAL CANDLE

If the congregation is processing into the church from outdoors, the second raising of the candle may be held at the entrance door. If the people are already in the sanctuary, the paschal candle may be elevated midway of the aisle.

Cantor: Christ our light.

People: **Thanks be to God.**

THIRD RAISING OF THE PASCHAL CANDLE

The paschal candle may be raised the third time at its stand in the center of the chancel, between the table and the congregation.

Cantor: Christ our light.

People: **Thanks be to God.**

The paschal candle may be placed in its stand.

EASTER PROCLAMATION A

While the congregation remains standing, holding their candles, a cantor may sing or say the following ancient Easter hymn, "Exsultet." (The indented verses may be omitted to shorten the hymn.)

Cantor: Rejoice, heavenly powers!
      Sing, choirs of angels!
      Jesus Christ, our light, is risen!
      Sound the trumpet of salvation!

      Rejoice, O earth, in shining splendor,
      Radiant in the brightness of your Sovereign!

      Christ has conquered! Glory fills you!
      Night vanishes for ever!

Rejoice, O servant church! Exult in glory!
The risen Savior shines upon you!
Let this place resound with joy,
Echoing the mighty song of all God's people!

> My dearest friends,
> Standing with me in this holy light,
> Join me in asking God's mercy,
> That God may give an unworthy pastor
> Grace to sing these Easter praises.

Cantor: God be with you.

People: **And also with you.**

Cantor: Lift up your hearts.

People: **We lift them to God.**

Cantor: Let us give thanks to God Most High.

People: **It is right to give God thanks and praise.**

Cantor: It is truly right
That with full hearts and minds and voices
We should praise you, the unseen God,
The eternal Creator,
And your only begotten one,
Our Savior Jesus Christ.

For Christ has ransomed us
With his blood
And for our salvation
Has paid you the cost
Of Adam and Eve's sin!

This is our Passover feast,
When Christ, the true lamb, is slain,
Whose blood consecrates the homes
Of all believers.

This is the night
When first you saved our ancestors:
You freed the people of Israel
From their slavery
And led them dry-shod through the sea.

This is the night when the pillar of fire
Destroyed the shadows of sin!

This is the night when Christians everywhere,
Washed clean of sin
And freed from all defilement,
Are restored to grace
And to grow together in holiness.

This is the night when Jesus Christ
Broke the chains of death
And rose triumphant from the grave.

> O God, how wonderful your care for us!
> How boundless your merciful love!
> To ransom a slave
> You gave your only child.

> O happy fault,
> O necessary sin of Eve and Adam,
> That gained for us so great a redeemer!
> Most blessed of all nights, chosen by God
> To see Christ rising from the dead!

> Of this night scripture says:
> "The night will be as clear as day;
> It will become my light, my joy."

> The power of this holy night
> Dispels all evil,
> Washes guilt away,
> Restores lost innocence,
> Brings mourners joy;
> It casts out hatred, brings peace,
> And humbles earthly pride.

> Night truly blessed
> When heaven is wedded to earth
> And humanity is reconciled with God!

Therefore, gracious Creator,
In the joy of this night,
Receive our evening sacrifice of praise,
Your church's solemn offering.

> Accept this Easter candle,
> A flame divided but undimmed,
> A pillar of fire that glows to your honor, O God.
>
> Let it mingle with the lights of heaven
> And continue bravely burning
> To dispel the shadows of this night!
> May the Morning Star which never sets
> Find this flame still burning:
> Christ, that Morning Star,
> Who came back from the dead,
> And shed your peaceful light
> On all creation,
> Your only begotten one
> Who lives and reigns for ever.

People: **Amen.**

EASTER PROCLAMATION B

(An alternate to the use of "Exsultet")

Reader: Rejoice, heavenly choirs of angels.

People: **Rejoice, all creation around God's throne.**

Reader: Christ has conquered! Glory fills you!

People: **Darkness vanishes for ever.**

Followed by this hymn, to the tune "Tallis Canon":

> All praise to thee, my God, this night,
> For all the blessings of the light!
> Keep me, O keep me, King of kings,
> Beneath thine own almighty wings!
>
> O Christ, who art the Light and Day,
> Thou drivest death and night away!
> We know thee as the Light of light,
> Illuminating mortal sight.
>
> Teach us to live, that we may dread
> The grave as little as our bed;
> Teach us to die, that so we may
> Rise glorious at the judgment day.

Praise God, from whom all blessings flow;
Praise God, all creatures here below;
Praise God above, ye heavenly host;
Praise Father, Son, and Holy Ghost.

At the conclusion of the Easter proclamation, if individual candles have been provided for the congregation, ask the people to extinguish their candles and be seated. As this is done, only those electric lights necessary for reasonable vision should be turned on.

SERVICE OF THE WORD

The number of Old Testament lessons traditionally read for the vigil varies from two to twelve. The reading of Exodus 14 is always included. Four Old Testament lessons with accompanying prayers are suggested here.

Other lessons traditionally used are:
    Genesis 7:1–5, 11–18; 8:6–18; 9:8–13 (Noah and the flood);
    Ezekiel 36:16–17a, 18–28 (a new heart and a new spirit);
    Ezekiel 37:1–14 (the valley of the dry bones);
    Jonah 3:1–10 (our missionary calling);
    Zephaniah 3:14–20 (the gathering of God's people);
    Isaiah 54:5–14 (love calls us back);
    Isaiah 4:2–6 (hope for Israel); and
    Daniel 3:1–29 (song of three men).

It is customary for certain psalms or canticles to be sung following particular readings. These have been noted.

The people serving as readers may stand around the paschal candle and move after each reading so that the one reading faces the congregation and is flanked by the other readers. The readers may hold their candles during the readings.

GREETING

A leader may introduce the Service of the Word in these or similar words.

Leader: Dear brothers and sisters in Christ:
        We have begun our solemn vigil.
        As we watch and wait,
        let us listen to the word of God,
        recalling God's saving acts throughout history
        and how, in the fullness of time,

God's Word became flesh and dwelt among us:
Jesus Christ, our Redeemer!

People: **We do not live by bread alone,
but by every word that proceeds from the mouth of God.**

OLD TESTAMENT READINGS

FIRST LESSON

The Creation Genesis 1:1—2:3 or Genesis 1:1, 26–31,
Psalm 33:1–11 or Psalm 46:5–10

COLLECT

Leader: Let us pray.

All: **Almighty God, who wonderfully created,
yet more wonderfully restored,
the dignity of human nature,
grant that we may share the divine life
of the one who came to share our humanity:
Jesus Christ, our Redeemer.
Amen.**

SECOND LESSON

Abraham's and Sarah's Faithfulness Genesis 22:1–18
Psalm 33:12–22 or Psalm 16

COLLECT

Leader: Let us pray.

All: **Gracious God of all believers,
through Sarah's and Abraham's trustful obedience
you made known your covenant love
to our ancestors and to us.
By the grace of Christ's trustful obedience,
even unto death,
fulfill in your church and in all creation
your promise of a new covenant,
written not on tablets of stone,
but on the tablets of human hearts;
through Jesus Christ our Savior.
Amen.**

THIRD LESSON

Israel's Deliverance at the Red Sea Exodus 14:15—15:1
    or Exodus 14:21–29
The Song of Moses Exodus 15:1–19

COLLECT

Leader: Let us pray.

All: God our Savior,
              even today we see the wonders of miracles
              you worked long ago.
              You once saved a single nation from slavery,
              and now you offer that salvation to all
              through the grace of baptism.
              May all the peoples of the world become true
              daughters and sons of Abraham and Sarah
              and be made worthy of the heritage of Israel;
              through Jesus Christ,
              our only mediator and advocate.
              Amen.

FOURTH LESSON

Salvation Offered Freely to All Isaiah 55:1–11
The First Song of Isaiah 12:2–6

COLLECT

Leader: Let us pray.

All: Eternal God, you created all things
              by the power of your Word,
              and you renew the earth by your Spirit.
              Give now the water of life
              to all who thirst for you,
              and nourish with the spiritual food of bread and wine
              all who hunger for you,
              that our lives on earth may bear the abundant fruit
              of your heavenly reign;
              through Jesus Christ,

the firstborn from the dead,
who, with you and the Holy Spirit,
lives and reigns for ever.
Amen.

ACT OF PRAISE

The readers may return to their places, and all may stand to sing a hymn of praise.

During the singing of this hymn, the candles on or near the table may be lighted, additional electric lights may be turned on, and the church bell may be pealed joyfully. In some congregations, it is the custom not to use the organ until this hymn.

NEW TESTAMENT READINGS

The people may be seated. A collect may be said prior to the Epistle.

EPISTLE LESSON

Our Death and Resurrection in Jesus Christ Romans 6:3–11
Psalm 114, Psalm 118, or another hymn

The congregation stands for the reading of the gospel suggested in the ecumenical lectionary. The reading may be introduced by singing or saying an alleluia and/or "Glory to you, O Christ." It may be followed by "Praise to you, O Christ" and/or an alleluia.

GOSPEL LESSON

Christ's Resurrection
    Year A: Matthew 28:1–10
    Year B: Mark 16:1–8
    Year C: Luke 24:1–12

SERMON (MAY BE OMITTED)

HYMN

The congregation stands for a hymn introducing the baptism theme.

SERVICE OF WATER

This service is both for baptism and the renewal of baptismal vows. If there are no candidates for baptism, the baptism and prayer for the baptized are omitted.

Other suitable baptismal rites may be found in other places in this volume.

GREETING

A pitcher of water and one or more basins may be placed where they may be seen by all. Sprigs of pine or another native tree may be placed near the pitcher and basins.

The one presiding, near the pitcher of water, may lead the people in a responsive greeting, using the following or other suitable words. The people may be seated.

Leader: Dear friends,
on this night of prayerful vigil
as we come to this living water,
let us recall the meaning of baptism.

For just as the body is one
and has many members,
and all the members of the body,
though many, are one body,
so it is with Christ.

People: **For by one Spirit
we are baptized into one body—
Jews or Greeks, slaves or free—
and all were made to drink of one Spirit.**

Leader: Now you are the body of Christ
and individually members of it.

BLESSING OF WATER

One of the following prayers or a similar one may be said.

PRAYER A

Leader: Let us pray.
We thank you, God for the gift of creation

called forth by your saving Word.
Before the world had shape and form,
your Spirit moved over the waters.
Out of the waters of the deep,
you formed the firmament
and brought forth the earth
to sustain all life.

In the time of Noah,
you washed the earth with the waters of the flood,
and your ark of salvation bore a new beginning.

In the time of Moses, your people Israel
passed through the Red Sea waters
from slavery to freedom
and crossed the flowing Jordan
to enter the promised land.
In the fullness of time, you sent Jesus Christ
who was nurtured in the water of Mary's womb.

Jesus was baptized by John in the water of the Jordan,
became living water to a woman at the Samaritan well,
washed the feet of the disciples,
and sent them forth to baptize all the nations
by water and the Holy Spirit.

*As the following words are spoken, the water may be poured into the basins,
or dipped from the baptistry into the basins.*

Bless by your Holy Spirit, gracious God, this water,
that by it we may be reminded of our baptism
into Jesus Christ
and that by the power of your Holy Spirit
we may be kept faithful until you receive us at last
in your eternal home.

All: **Glory to you, eternal God,
the one who was, and is, and shall always be,
world without end. Amen.**

PRAYER B

Leader: Eternal God, on this night of watching and waiting,
we offer our prayers to you.

People: **Be with us**
as we recall the wonder
of our creation
and the greater wonder
of our redemption.

As the following words are spoken, the water may be poured into the basins.

Leader: Bless this water.
It makes the seeds to grow.
It refreshes us and makes us clean.

People: **You have made of it**
a servant of your loving-kindness:
Through water you set your people free
and quenched their thirsts in the desert.

Leader: With water, the prophets announced a new covenant
that you would make with all humanity.

People: **By water, made holy by Christ in the Jordan,**
you made our sinful nature new in the bath
that gives rebirth.

Leader: Let this water remind us of our baptism.

People: **Let us share the joy of our brothers and sisters**
throughout the world who are baptized this Easter;
through Jesus Christ our risen Savior. Amen.

BAPTISMAL VOWS

*The congregation stands. The following affirmation of faith in question form,
a statement of faith or covenant, or another form prepared for the occasion
may be used. The questions are addressed to the congregation as individuals
for affirmation of each person's baptism. Candidates for baptism may come
to be near the paschal candle. First, they face away from the light. After
renouncing evil they turn to face the light.*

Leader: Let each one who believes renounce evil.
Do you renounce evil, its service and its works?

People: **I do.**

*The leader has the candidates for baptism turn to face the light of the paschal
candle.*

Leader: Do you believe in God?

People: **I believe in God, the creator of heaven and earth.**

Leader: Do you believe in Jesus Christ?

People: **I believe in Jesus Christ, the only one begotten of God before all worlds.**

Leader: Do you believe in the Holy Spirit?

People: **I believe in God, the Holy Spirit.**

Leader: Will you continue in the apostles' teaching and community, in the breaking of bread, and in prayer?

People: **I will, with God's help.**

Leader: Will you strive for justice and peace among all people, respecting the dignity of every human being?

People: **I will, with God's help.**

BLESSING OF THE PEOPLE

The congregation stands. In these or similar words, a leader may invoke God's blessing upon all who have renewed their vows.

Leader: Let us pray.

Eternal God,
you have come to us in Jesus Christ,
given us new birth by water
and the Holy Spirit,
and forgiven all our sins.
Bless us now with the grace we need
to fulfill what we have promised.

People: **Keep us faithful to our Savior Jesus Christ,
for ever and ever.
Amen.**

At this time, candidates for baptism go to the baptistry. While the choir sings an anthem (such as one based on Ephesians 4:4–6) or as the congregation sings a hymn, leaders may move among the congregation and sprinkle the people with water from the basins using the sprigs from a tree. The mood appropriate for the occasion is joy.

At the conclusion of the sprinkling, the leaders may return to the baptistry and pour the remaining water from the basins into the baptistry in full view of the people.

THE BAPTISM

Each candidate enters the baptistry to be immersed.

Pastor: Name, I baptize you in the name of the Father, the Son, and the Holy Spirit.
or
Name, you are baptized in the name of the Father, and of the Son, and of the Holy Spirit. Amen.

PRAYER FOR THE BAPTIZED

The following prayer is to be said after the last candidate is baptized.

Pastor: O Holy One, you who create and nurture the faithful,
including these who are newly baptized,
we give you thanks for grace
acknowledged here today in water
and the Holy Spirit.
Embrace us all as sons and daughters
in the one household of your love.
Grant us grace to receive, nurture, and befriend
(this new member/these new members) of the body of Christ.

People: **Give to the newly baptized:**
Strength for life's journey,
courage in time of suffering,
the joy of faith, the freedom
of love and the hope of new life;
Through Jesus Christ, who makes us one.
Amen.
or
Pastor: Creator God, we thank you that by water and the Holy Spirit,
You have bestowed upon these your servants the forgiveness of sin.
And have raised them to the new life of grace.

Sustain them, O Lord, in your Holy Spirit.
Give them an inquiring and discerning heart,
the courage to will and to persevere,
a Spirit to know you and to love you
and the gift of joy and wonder in all your works.
Amen.

A hymn of joy may be sung.

SERVICE OF THE BREAD AND CUP

OFFERING

While the offering is being received, an Easter hymn or anthem may be sung. During this time, the table is prepared. The gifts of bread and wine are brought forward from the congregation or from a nearby table. Also, oil and communion cups of milk and honey are brought to the table. During this offering the newly baptized members return to the sanctuary and are seated in a reserved section at the front. When the table is ready, the pastor says:

Beloved in Christ!
People shall be gathered from north and south,
from east and west,
to feast at the heavenly banquet of the Lord.
Christ, our Paschal Lamb has been sacrificed. Alleluia!

WELCOME OF THE NEWLY BAPTIZED TO THE TABLE

The pastor addresses the newly baptized.

Pastor: Today begins your walk in the way of Christ's resurrection. We anoint you with the oil of thanksgiving and pray that the Holy Spirit sustain you in your life of ministry.

The elders come to the table to get oil and take oil to the baptized. They make a sign of the cross in oil on the forehead of each newly baptized person. The elders then lay hands on the heads of the newly baptized while the pastor prays the following or a similar prayer.

O Lord, God,
you count these your servants worthy of forgiveness of sins
by the bath of baptism.

Make them worthy to be filled with your Holy Spirit
and send upon them your grace,
that they may serve you according to your will.
We pray in the name of Jesus Christ. Amen.

Throughout your life, you are to be fed from this table that
God's grace may continue to flourish in your life.

At this table Easter is celebrated. Christ, our Paschal Lamb,
has been sacrificed. He has been raised from the dead that we
might live. He will call us to eternal life.

As Jesus ate the passover meal with his disciples, he remembered their ancestors, newborn to freedom, moving toward
the land of milk and honey. Drink now this milk, the food of
babies. Drink now this honey. Savor the sweetness of God's
promise.

The elders serve cups of mixed milk and honey to the newly baptized.

GREETING OF THE NEWLY BAPTIZED AND PASSING THE PEACE

*The pastor invites the congregation to greet the newly baptized and each
other with the passing of the peace.*

PRAYER AT THE TABLE[24]

Pastor: Holy god, from the beginning of creation you have
demonstrated your will to bring life out of death.

People: **Alleluia!**

Single Voices

First: When the fierce, primeval sea
raged against your ordered world,
you made the waters to be
the source of fertility and life.

Second: When Abraham raised the knife
to sacrifice his only son,
you trapped a ram in the thicket
to be the sacrifice and to save the boy.

Third: When the people of Israel
were threatened by the angel of death,
you commanded them to paint their door posts

with the blood of the lamb,
and their children did not die.

Fourth: When the valley was filled with dry bones,
you sent the prophet to speak your word.
Sinews came upon the bones
covering them with flesh,
and they stood on their feet and lived.

Fifth: When the women came to the tomb
prepared to anoint the body
and abandon all hope,
you rolled away the stone
and revealed the Lord Jesus
risen from the dead.

People: **Holy God, Glory to you!**
Alleluia!

Pastor: We give thanks to you, God our Savior,
that you transform death into life,

People: **And that the body and blood of Jesus,**
put to death upon the cross,
becomes the means of life for us.

Pastor: We praise you, Holy God,
that over this bread and wine
your Holy Spirit speaks again
the transforming words of Jesus:
This is my body. This is my blood.

People: **Release your life-giving power**
as we partake of the loaf and cup.

Pastor: May we who live in the valley of the shadow of
death be raised to renewed life and witness.

People: **Inspire us to work for that day**
when Christ shall come again
and the whole world shall be raised to glory.
Through the same Jesus Christ,
with you and the Holy Spirit,
one God now and forever. Amen.

Receiving Bread and Communion Wine

The elders serve the newly baptized first.

Prayer After Communion

Women: Liberating God,
from death, you brought Jesus into new life.

Men: From bondage to sin, you bring us to abundant life.

All: **Now from this feast of bread and wine raise us to speak
your name in power and to live your way in peace. Amen.**

Dismissal

A closing hymn is sung.

The Benediction

Great God of peace,
you brought again from the dead
our Lord Jesus Christ,
the great shepherd of the sheep.
By the blood of the eternal covenant,
equip us with everything good,
that we may do your will,
working through us,
all that is pleasing in your sight.
Through the same Jesus Christ,
to whom be glory for ever and ever. Amen.
(Adapted from Hebrews 13:20–21)

PART TWO

Belonging

BELONGING

Introduction

This section of the book shifts focus. In Part One, the services express baptism as the sacrament of initiation into the life of the Christian community. A second theme—that baptism expresses the continuing life of that community—is muted. In Part Two, the emphasis is reversed. These rites and ceremonies are based on the presupposition that the church is a community. The liturgies included here come at points when people and the church open wide their arms in love and acceptance. Although these services also include initiatory aspects, these aspects are less important than the solidarity of the church and its people in times of change.

One such time is the birth or adoption of a child. At this moment parents and other members of the family and circle of friends experience an unusual openness to God and desire to ritualize their life. There is a kind of natural religious response to the new life. Sometimes the people surrounding the new child have a limited commitment to the religious life but still want to gather with representatives of religion to give thanks. Among other people there is an openness to a more serious engagement with the church's sacramental life and process of nurture. In some churches these desires are fulfilled in infant baptism; yet even in these churches a pre-baptismal act of thanksgiving often is desirable. Churches that delay baptism until preadolescence are especially in need of a way to embrace young children in their life.

Services for use with infants usually focus around three themes. The first is thanksgiving to God for the birth or adoption of the child and for the new challenge that has come to the family. The second element is intercession. People ask God to help them with the demanding task that now is theirs, the task of rearing this child in ways that are good. The third theme is accepting responsibility for the care, nurture, and religious guidance to be given to the child.

Another time of beginning is when a person baptized in infancy is ready to affirm vows on his or her own behalf. This affirmation of baptism becomes the personal appropriation of what was said and done at a time before the baptized can remember. The service of the affirmation of baptismal vows begins with the renewing of the confession of faith in Jesus Christ. It continues with the prayer for the Holy Spirit and concludes with their being welcomed more fully into the life of the church. This first affirmation of baptismal vows is the center of what churches have in the past called the service of confirmation.

There are other occasions when people desire to be put in touch again with the power of their baptism. Times of great stress that lead to renewal or a kind of birth of Christian commitment that is so intense as to be a new beginning are examples. Even in these times of intensification, we should remember that baptism itself is not to be repeated. In baptism, God is the one who acts. What God does is forgive sin and incorporate the newly baptized into the ongoing body of Christ. If God has done these things once and for all, then the church has no right to act as though God's action has been set aside. To go through the form of baptism a second time is an empty action. The church also resists rebaptism because such an action is an affront to the integrity of other churches. When any church baptizes, even in a way that may differ from the way we baptize, that action still is Christian baptism. For any church to rebaptize someone whom another church has baptized, is a great breach of the oneness of the body of Christ. The church is one, despite its highly divided historical form, and despite the widely differing forms of baptism.

Two services are presented for use when a child comes into a home. The first one, When Life Begins, is taken from a worship book published by the Presbyterian Church in Canada. Much of the content of the service is adapted slightly from a similar order published by the Anglican Church of Canada. It is a simple service of thanksgiving and petition suitable for use by any family when new life enters the home. The text leaves open the question of the family's relationship to the faith community and its intentions concerning the future.

The second service is one prepared by the Commission on Worship of The Consultation on Church Union. It is similar to services published by several churches and used among Disciples for the last half century. This service of thanksgiving is more complex than the earlier one because it assumes Christian faith within the family and the intention of the family to rear the child as a Christian.

Both of these services are appropriate for use by Disciples. They acknowledge in suitable ways that a child has entered into the Christian home and into the faith community of the congregation. These services provide a way to give an appropriate ritualization to this important beginning of life.

The above occasions are designed around the pastoral needs of individuals or small groups. It is also appropriate that congregations renew baptismal vows. Of course, every baptism invites members of the congregation to remember their own baptism and to renew their baptismal vows. Every celebration of communion is also a way of renewing the meaning of baptism. Yet there are also occasions when the congregation in a more deliberate way calls attention to baptism as the foundation for its life. The anniversary of the congregation is an example. Another example is a time when officers are commissioned for their work. Because the life of the church is rooted in baptism, then services for the renewing of baptismal vows make sense.

The chapter entitled "Becoming Faithful...Becoming Christian" contains materials that are both worship and education. It includes an extended program of nurture and instruction in the faith. At pivotal points in the process, participants take part in brief acts of worship in the congregation's Sunday worship. Ordinarily these times when worship, education, and evangelism come together are Advent and Lent.

When Life Begins[25]

As each gift of life is received into family and church, let prayers of thanksgiving and intercession be offered for the child, the parents, and all whose lives are touched by the event. Some prayers will be offered informally by individuals in the presence of mother and child. A prayer may be included in the prayers of thanksgiving and intercession during worship on the following Sunday. On other occasions, a brief service may be held in the hospital soon after delivery, or in the home with other members of the family when the newly born or adopted child has come home.

A brief service for use in hospital or home may be outlined as follows.

> Greeting
> Adoration
> Readings from Scripture
> Prayers of Thanksgiving
> Prayers of Intercession
> The Lord's Prayer
> Ascription of Glory
> Benediction

PRAYERS AND READINGS

A CHRISTIAN GREETING

> The Lord be with you.
> **And also with you.**

A PRAYER OF ADORATION

> Gracious God:
> like a mother who nurtures her children
> you have cared for us;
> like a father you have called us by name
> and claimed us as your own;
> you have loved us into being,
> placed us in human families,
> and blessed us on our journey.
> By the presence of your Spirit
> you confirm our joy in this moment.

You, O God, are the source of all life
and we praise your holy name;
through Jesus Christ our Savior. Amen.

SOME SUGGESTED READINGS

A brief comment or a moment for silent reflection may follow the reading from Scripture.

Psalm 8
Psalm 68:4–6b, 19, 35
Psalm 103:1–5, 13–14, 17–18, 22
Psalm 116:1–2, 5, 12–13, 18–19
Deuteronomy 6:4–9
I Samuel 1:9–11, 20–28, 2:26
Mark 9:33–37
Mark 10:13–16
Luke 2:22–33, (34–35), 52

THANKSGIVING AFTER DELIVERY

Gracious God, creator and sustainer of all:
we praise you for calling *Name* and *Name*
to share in your creative action
through the wondrous mystery of childbirth.
We give thanks that *Name* has been brought
safely through her time of pregnancy and labor.
Strengthen her now
that she might nourish and nurture this child,
sharing with you in the joy of creative love.
We ask this in the name of the One who was born of a woman,
Jesus Christ our Redeemer.
Amen.

A PRAYER FOR PARENTS

Gracious God, our creator, redeemer, and sustainer;
we thank you for the gift of this child
entrusted now to the care of *Name* and *Name*.
May they be patient and understanding,
ready to guide, quick to forgive.
Through your grace given to them,
may *this child* know your love
and learn to love your world,

and the whole family of your children;
through Jesus Christ our Savior.
Amen.

A Prayer for Use by Parents

Gracious God, giver of all life,
we thank you for calling us
to share in your work of creation,
and especially for giving us this child, *Name*.
Help us to show *him/her* such faith and love
that *he/she* may daily grow in grace
and live to serve you and your people,
through Jesus Christ our Lord.
Amen.

A Prayer for the Home

Lord Jesus Christ,
who shared in Nazareth the life of an earthly home:
dwell, we pray, in this home.
Give to *Name, Name,* and *Name*
the grace to serve each other as you have served.
Grant that by deed and word they may be witnesses
to your saving love among those with whom they live.
May all who live here learn to live as members
of your commonwealth on earth.
We ask this in your holy name.
Amen.

For Use by Parents When a Child Has a Disability

O God, creator of us all:
we give you thanks for this child
committed now into our care.
Grant to us hearts that are understanding and accepting;
give to us the gifts of courage and patience
to face the challenges ahead.
In the midst of our disappointment and fear,
may your love for us show forth in our love for *him/her*.
Help us to create an atmosphere in which *he/she*
may live a life of dignity and worth.

Through Jesus Christ, the One who shared
our human journey and strengthens us on the way.
Amen.

FOR AN ADOPTED CHILD

Gracious God:
you have adopted us as your children
calling us the heirs of your commonwealth.
We rejoice in your loving kindness.
We give you thanks for *Name*
who has come to bless this family
and for *Name* and *Name*
who have welcomed *him/her* as their own.
By the power of your Holy Spirit
fill their home with love, trust, and understanding,
that they may grow together in faith and maturity,
through Jesus Christ our Savior.
Amen.

THE LORD'S PRAYER

Our Father in heaven,
hallowed be your name,
your kingdom come,
your will be done,
on earth as in heaven.
Give us today our daily bread.
Forgive us our sins
as we forgive those who sin against us.
Save us from the time of trial
and deliver us from evil.
For the kingdom, the power and the glory are yours
now and forever. Amen.

AN ASCRIPTION OF GLORY

All glory be to you, O God,
whose power working in us can do infinitely more
than we can ask or imagine.
Glory be to you, O God,
from generation to generation, in the church
and in Christ Jesus, for ever and ever. Amen.

(Adapted from Ephesians 3:20.)

A BENEDICTION

> The grace of the Lord Jesus Christ,
> and the love of God,
> and the communion of the Holy Spirit
> be with you all. Amen.
> > *(2 Corinthians 13:13)*
> *or*

THE AARONIC BLESSING

> The Lord bless you and keep you.
> The Lord be kind and gracious to you.
> The Lord look upon you with favor
> and give you peace. Amen.
> > *(Adapted from Numbers 6:24–26)*

Thanksgiving for the Birth or Adoption of a Child[26]

This order is intended primarily for use within a regular, full service of worship. When conducted apart from that context, appropriate modifications may be made.

One or more of the following scripture passages may be used in the Liturgy of the Word, if this precedes the order, or at some suitable point within the order.

Deuteronomy 6:4–7.
> *Diligently teach your children.*

Deuteronomy 31:12–13.
> *Do...this...that your children may hear and learn.*

1 Samuel 1:9–11, 20–28; 2:26.
> *The birth and presentation of Samuel.*

Psalm 8.
> *"O Lord, our Sovereign, how majestic is your name in all the earth."*

Psalm 78:1–7.
> *"Tell to the coming generation the glorious deeds of the LORD."*

Matthew 18:1–4.
Those who humble themselves like children will be greatest.

Mark 10:13–16.
Jesus blesses the children.

Luke 2:22–32; 52.
The presentation of Jesus in the temple.

The order may begin with this presentation:

Members of Christ's family, I present to you *Name* and *Name* together with *Name* whose coming into their home they now acknowledge with gratitude and faith.

Then the pastor says:

Within the family of Christ, the birth or adoption of a child is an occasion for thanksgiving. Life is God's gift, and children are a heritage from the Lord. Because God has favored us through the coming of this child, let us offer our praise.

A hymn of praise, psalm, or canticle may be sung.

For the birth of a child, the following or another prayer is offered.

O God, as a mother comforts her children,
you strengthen, sustain, and provide for us.
We come before you with gratitude
for the gift of this child,
for the joy that has come into this family,
and for the grace with which you surround them and all of us.
As a father cares for his children,
so you continually look upon us
with compassion and goodness.
Pour out your Spirit.
Enable your servants to abound in love,
and establish our homes in holiness;
through Jesus Christ our Lord.
Amen.

For the adoption of a child, the following or another prayer is offered.

O God, you have adopted all of us as your children.
We give thanks to you for the child

who has come to bless this family
and for the parents who have welcomed
this child as their own.
By the power of your Holy Spirit,
fill their home with love, trust, and understanding;
through Jesus Christ our Lord.
Amen.

The pastor now asks:

What name have you given this child?

Those presenting the child respond.

However, if the name is to be offered as a part of this order, the pastor instead asks:

What name do you now give this child?

Those presenting the child may place their hands upon the child. They respond,

We name you *Name*.

The pastor then says to the family:

In accepting *Name* as a gift from God,
you also acknowledge your faith in Jesus Christ
and the responsibility that God places upon you.

The members of the family respond saying or repeating after the pastor:

We receive *Name*
from the hand of a loving Creator.
With humility and hope
we accept the obligation that is ours,
to love and nurture *her/him*
and to lead *her/him* to Christian faith
by our teaching and example.
We ask for the power of the Holy Spirit
and the support of the church
that we may be good stewards
of this gift of life.

The pastor then says to the congregation:

> The church is the family of Christ, the community in which
> we grow in faith and commitment.

The congregation responds:

> **We rejoice to take *Name* under our care.**
> **We seek God's grace to be a community**
> **in which the gospel is truly proclaimed to all.**
> **We will support you**
> **and minister with you**
> **as workers together in Christ Jesus**
> **and heirs of his promise.**

The pastor takes the child and says:

> *Name*, may the eternal God bless you
> and watch over you.
> May Jesus Christ incorporate you
> into his death and resurrection through baptism.
> May the Holy Spirit sanctify you
> and bring you to life everlasting.

The pastor returns the child to the family.
The pastor then offers this or another prayer:

> Gracious God,
> from whom every family in heaven and on earth is named:
> Out of the treasures of your glory
> strengthen us through your Spirit.
> Help us joyfully to nurture *Name*
> within your church.
> Bring *her/him* by grace to baptism and Christian maturity,
> that Christ may dwell in *her/his* heart through faith.
> Give power to *Name* and to us,
> that with all your people
> we may grasp the breadth and length,
> the height and depth of Christ's love.
> Enable us to know this love,
> though it is beyond knowledge,
> and to be filled with your own fullness;
> through Jesus Christ our Lord.
> Amen.

If the Lord's Prayer is not used at another point in the service, it may be prayed by all here.

The pastor may conclude the order by saying:

> Glory to God, who by the power at work among us
> is able to do far more than we can ask or imagine.
> Glory be given to this God
> from generation to generation
> in the church and in Christ Jesus for ever!
> Amen.

Affirmation of
the Baptismal Covenant[27]

This order is normally used as a part of the Sunday service of the congregation. It takes place after the liturgy of the Word, which includes the reading of one or more passages of scripture, a sermon, and the prayers of the people.

If it is desired to use scripture readings thematically related to this note, the following are appropriate:

Deuteronomy 30:15–20
> *I have set before you life and death; therefore choose life.*

Isaiah 61:1–9
> *The Spirit of the Lord has anointed me to proclaim liberty.*

Jeremiah 31:31–34
> *I will make a new covenant upon their hearts.*

Ezekiel 37:1–10
> *Can these dry bones live?*

Zephaniah 3:12–20
> *Do not fear, O Zion, the Lord is in your midst.*

Psalm 23
> *The Lord is my shepherd.*

Psalm 27
The Lord is my light and my salvation.

Romans 8:18–27
The Lord helps us in our weakness.

Romans 12:1–8
Present your bodies as a living sacrifice to God.

Ephesians 4:7, 11-16
Grace was given to each according to the measure of Christ.

1 Peter 2:4–10
You are a chosen race, a royal priesthood, God's own people.

Matthew 5:1–12
The Beatitudes

Matthew 16:24–27
Deny yourself, and take up your cross and follow me.

Luke 4:16–21
Jesus reads Isaiah in the synagogue at Nazareth.

John 3:15–21
God so loved the world. Whosoever does what is true comes to the light.

Following the liturgy of the Word those who wish to affirm their baptismal covenant (together with their sponsors)[28] are presented to the congregation. The pastor says:

These members of the family of Christ who have been baptized by water and the Holy Spirit now come to confess the faith, declare the promises, and accept the responsibilities of baptism.

The pastor then addresses the candidates:

Brothers and sisters in Christ: In the sacrament of holy baptism our Savior Jesus Christ has received you and made you members of his body the church. You share our life in Christ. You have studied the Word of God and been instructed in the practice of the Christian faith. (You have been nourished at the Lord's Table.)

When this order is used for the renewal of the baptismal covenant by the entire congregation, the presentation is omitted and the presiding pastor addresses the congregation:

Brothers and sisters in Christ: In the sacrament of holy baptism our Lord Jesus Christ has received us and made us members of his body the church. We share life in Christ and have been nourished at the Lord's Table. Let us this day renew the covenant of our baptism and commit ourselves to the responsibilities of our service to Christ.

Pastor: Do you now affirm your baptismal covenant?

Answer: **I do.**

Pastor: Do you renounce all the forces of evil in whatever guise they present themselves?

Answer: **I do.**

Pastor: Do you commit yourself(selves) to Jesus Christ and his service in the world?

Answer: **I do and with God's grace I will follow him as my Redeemer and the ruler of my life.**

The pastor may invite the congregation to join with those affirming their baptismal covenant in one of the forms following:

(1)   Do you believe in the one God, creator of all things?

I believe.

And in Jesus Christ, God's only begotten one, redeemer of the world?

I believe.

And in the Holy Spirit, who unites the Church in love?

I believe.

or

(2)   **I believe in God, the Father almighty, creator of heaven and earth.**

I believe in Jesus Christ, God's only Son, our Lord,
who was conceived by the Holy Spirit,
born of the Virgin Mary,
suffered under Pontius Pilate,
was crucified, died, and was buried;
he descended to the dead.
On the third day he rose again;
he ascended into heaven,
he is seated at the right hand of the Father,
and he will come to judge the living and the dead.

I believe in the Holy Spirit,
the holy catholic church,
the communion of saints,
the forgiveness of sins,
the resurrection of the body,
and the life everlasting. Amen.

or

(3)   Do you believe in God the Father?

I believe in God, the Father almighty,
creator of heaven and earth.

Do you believe in Jesus Christ, the Son of God?

I believe in Jesus Christ, God's only Son, our Lord,
who was conceived by the Holy Spirit,
born of the Virgin Mary,
suffered under Pontius Pilate,
was crucified, died, and was buried;
he descended to the dead.
On the third day he rose again;
he ascended into heaven,
he is seated at the right hand of the Father,
and he will come to judge the living and the dead.

Do you believe in God the Holy Spirit?

I believe in the Holy Spirit,
the holy catholic church,
the communion of saints,
the forgiveness of sins,

the resurrection of the body,
and the life everlasting.
or

(4)   Do you believe in God the Creator, who has made you and all
       the world?

I believe.

Do you believe in God the Savior, who has redeemed you and
all humanity?

I believe.

Do you believe in God the Holy Spirit, who sanctifies you and
all the people of God?

I believe.

The presiding pastor then addresses the congregation:

Let us pray for our sisters and brothers who have affirmed
their baptismal covenant and committed themselves to Jesus
Christ.

All pray in silence. Then, the presiding pastor offers this prayer:

Almighty God, through water and the Holy Spirit
you have made us your sons and daughters,
brought us into your church,
filled us with your Holy Spirit,
and given us your promise of eternal life.
Renew in these your children
the covenant you made with *them* at *their* baptism.
Stir up in *them* the power of the Holy Spirit
and send *them* forth to perform the service
you set before them;
through Jesus Christ our Lord,
who lives and reigns with you and the Holy Spirit,
one God, now and for ever.
Amen.

*When the order is used for the renewal of the baptismal covenant by the entire
congregation, the invitation may be* Let us pray; us *and* our *may be
substituted for the italicized pronouns in the prayer. The laying on of hands
is omitted and exchange of the greeting of peace takes place at once.*

Hands are now laid in turn upon each as the pastor(s) say(s):

> Strengthen, O Lord, your servant *Name*
> with your Holy Spirit,
> empower *him/her* for your service,
> and sustain *him/her* all the days of *his/her* life.
> Amen.
>
> *or*
>
> *Name*, may Almighty God strengthen you
> in the gift of the Holy Spirit, deepen your faith,
> direct your life, empower you for service,
> give you patience in suffering,
> and bring you to everlasting life.
> Amen.

If the signing and sealing from An Order for the Celebration of Holy Baptism *is to take place, it follows here and its formula replaces that for the laying of hands, the pastor placing a hand on the head of each person and making the sign of the cross (using oil[29] prepared for this purpose, if desired), and saying:*

> *Name*, you are sealed by the Holy Spirit
> and marked with the sign of Christ's cross,
> that you may know him and the power of his resurrection,
> and the fellowship of his sufferings.

The pastor and members of the congregation exchange the greeting of peace with those who have affirmed their baptismal covenant.

The service continues with intercessions, including prayer by name for those who have affirmed their baptismal covenant, and with the celebration of the Lord's Supper.

BECOMING FAITHFUL...
BECOMING CHRISTIAN

A PROCESS OF NURTURE AND CELEBRATION IN PREPARATION FOR CHRISTIAN BAPTISM

Introduction

An examination of the New Testament church shows that two major issues were closely connected. The first centered around the evangelism of converts and their entrance into the Christian community. The second concern focused on the vitality and faithful witness of the Christian community to the gospel. In New Testament times Christian baptism and continuing faithfulness to the gospel were both important.

Today we continue to believe that the Christian community has a responsibility to be faithful to the mandate from Christ to "make disciples of all nations" (Matthew 28:19). It is our mission and our task to renew faithful discipleship in our congregational life and to evoke a committed response from others to Jesus Christ, the Light of the world.

Over the centuries, both Protestants and Roman Catholics have lost this sense of the involvement of the entire community in the process of Christian baptism. We have assumed that becoming a Christian is a matter of education. We take a class, read a book about the church or the Christian life, attend Bible study, all of which are pieces of the learning that must be integrated into the total fabric of life. A comprehensive process of Christian nurture in preparation for baptism includes all the components that make up the Christian life: worship, education, service, and fellowship.

Within the last twenty years, several church bodies have developed comprehensive programs that attempt to attend more faithfully to the process of Christian nurture for persons seeking baptism. The most notable is The Rite of Christian Initiation of Adults developed by the Roman Catholic Church in the 1970s. These systems carefully develop a method for the renewal of the congregation based upon the process of adult initiation.

109

The most important idea undergirding these comprehensive programs is that many people coming to the church have little knowledge of the gospel and Christian way of life. Therefore, an intensive program of nurture and instruction is necessary. A second undergirding idea is that becoming a follower of Jesus Christ is a public act and changes the character of one's life in a public way. For this reason the process of Christian nurture needs to be celebrated in acts of worship.

The fully developed process leading to baptism has three stages: (1) An introduction to the Christian community; (2) candidacy for baptism, and (3) incorporation into Christ. Each stage includes brief acts of worship that take place during the Sunday service. Ordinarily, the time during the service for these special rites is after the invitation to discipleship or prior to the prayers of intercession.

Before the stages begin, there is ordinarily a period of inquiry and evangelism in which individuals and the church community make contact for the first time. This might occur through the congregation's outreach and education or through the Sunday worship service. The three-stage program of nurture and celebration begins with the first stage, introduction, when an individual participates in educational programs of instruction or ministries of nurture within the local congregation, and more formally agrees to participate in the process of prayer, study, and spiritual discipline which lead to baptism. The second stage, candidacy, takes place during Lent or Advent and includes an educational process of Bible study, and the support of a Christian friend who agrees to share the journey toward baptism with the candidate. The third stage, incorporation, includes the process of ongoing renewal within the life of the congregation.

These stages and the recommended acts of worship are summarized below. The services follow in the next section.

STAGE ONE:
INTRODUCTION TO THE CHRISTIAN COMMUNITY

Purpose of this stage: To help learners discover in the Christian story the means of interpreting their own life stories.

Dates: A Sunday several weeks prior to the beginning of Lent or the beginning of Advent.

Acts of Worship:

Presentation of the Candidates:
Acceptance of the Gospel
Affirmation by the Congregation
The Prayers

A period of formal instruction and nurture follows.

STAGE TWO:
CANDIDACY FOR BAPTISM

Purpose of this stage: The deepening of the experience of God's love, faith in Jesus Christ, and power in the Holy Spirit.

Dates: The Sundays of Lent or of Advent and Christmastide.

Acts of Worship:

Enrollment: 1st Sunday in Lent; 1st Sunday in Advent.
Declarations of Faithfulness
Enrollment in the Book of Candidates for Baptism
Litany

Presentation of a Bible: 2nd Sunday in Lent; in Advent, combined with the Enrollment on the first Sunday.
Presentation of the Bible
Prayers

Prayer for New Life (Cleansing): 3rd Sunday in Lent; 2nd Sunday in Advent.
Celebration of God's Word
Declaration
Prayer
Blessing

Prayers for New Life (Illumination): 4th Sunday in Lent; 3rd Sunday in Advent.
Celebration of God's Word
Declaration
Prayer

Gesture: Touching the Ears and Eyes
Blessing

Prayers for New Life (Spiritual Renewal): 5th Sunday in Lent;
4th Sunday in Advent.
Celebration of God's Word
Declaration
Prayer
Gesture: Giving the Lord's Prayer and Saying It Together
Blessing

STAGE THREE:
INCORPORATION INTO CHRIST

Purpose of this stage: To be united with Christ in baptism and
joined to the church as a living member.

Acts of Worship:

Confession of Faith: Palm / Passion Sunday; Sunday after Christmas.
Declaration
Prayer
The Confession of Faith
The Blessing

Baptism: Easter; Sunday after Epiphany (Baptism of Jesus).

Rites and Texts

STAGE ONE:
INTRODUCTION TO THE CHRISTIAN COMMUNITY

Pastor (to all the candidates):
> You have followed God's light and truth and you are led to affirm your belief in the living God. As you begin your journey to Christian baptism and new life in Christ, make Christ and his teachings the pattern of your lives. Put on the mind of Christ and walk in his light. Love God and your neighbor, for this is Christ's command.
>
> Are you prepared to learn about Jesus Christ and life in the love of God to which he calls?

Candidates: **I am with God's help.**

Pastor: Will the congregation please stand.
How will you support and nurture these candidates as they begin the journey that leads to baptism?

People: **We will pray for them and send companions for them from our assembly. We welcome them into fellowship with our community of faith.**

Pastor: Will the sponsors please come forward and place your hand on your friend's shoulder to designate your promise to share the journey that leads to baptism. You are representatives of this community of faith. Are you ready to help these candidates discover and follow Jesus Christ?

Sponsors: **We are.**

Pastor: Let us pray:
God, you search and seek that which was lost.
You tenderly lead us home to you.
You call us each by name.

Be with those you have called this day that they may walk as children of the light:

We praise you, God, and we bless you.

All: **We praise you, God, and we bless you. Amen.**

Pastor: Let us pray for our sisters and brothers who begin their journey toward baptism and new life in Christ. God's loving guidance has always been with them, and now they acknowledge God's goodness. Let us pray that they may come to know, love, and serve God in fellowship with us, and with our Lord Jesus Christ. O God of love,

All: **Hear our prayer.**

Pastor: Creator God, we pray that they may see in our signs of unity and generosity, a faithful witness to your enduring love. O God of love,

All: **Hear our prayer.**

Pastor: Redeeming Christ, we pray that you may open our hearts and enable us all to be more responsive to your gospel of love made visible in lives of service to our neighbors. O God of love,

All: **Hear our prayer.**

Pastor: Sustaining and renewing Spirit, we pray that we may all become worthy of the promises of Christ as you descend upon our community. Fill us with your light and your peace. O God of love,

All: **Hear our prayer.**

Pastor (pray with hand outstretched as in a blessing):

Holy God, source of all life,
we are your daughters and sons,
created in your image,
molded and fashioned by your Spirit
to become one with Jesus, your son.
We ask your blessing on those
who have come to hear your Word.

May your power renew, your grace sustain,
and your love surround these friends
on their journey to faithful discipleship with Jesus Christ,
the light of the world.

All: Amen.

STAGE TWO:
CANDIDACY FOR BAPTISM

FIRST SUNDAY IN LENT OR ADVENT: ENROLLMENT

(After the enrollment, the candidates may sit in a designated place in the congregation with their nurturing team.)

Pastor: In our worship this morning, we pray for our friends *(give their names here)* who are preparing for Christian baptism.

Will the candidates please stand.

Holy God,
We present to your care our brothers and sisters
preparing for baptism.
Free them from the power of sin and the lure of evil.
You reached down to deliver your people, Israel.
You showed your power to save.
You spoke through the prophets to announce
your steadfast love for all creation
and your desire that all people return to you,
that your will might be accomplished on earth.
In your great love, you sent your Son Jesus,
showing us that your love conquers even death.
With your Spirit, you enable us to see
what no eye has seen and to hear what no ear has heard,
and you continue to bring us the good news
that we are your daughters and sons in Christ.
Set us free, we pray, that we might walk
in the light of the Lord.
We pray this in the name of Jesus,
the Christ of God. Amen.

(This prayer is also used for the 2nd Sunday in Lent.)

(To the candidates:)

The weeks of Lent (Advent) are a time of spiritual preparation for you. You await the time when you are received fully into the Christian community through the waters of Christian baptism. This is a time of prayer and fasting, of

seeking the purification of the Spirit, who was with Jesus
when he was tempted in the wilderness. It is a time to be
aware of the presence of God who has called you to new
wholeness in Christ Jesus.

Today, we ask that you pray for the grace of Christ as you
renounce evil and its effects in your life.

Do you renounce evil in all its forms and promise to
worship God alone?

Candidates: **I do.**

Pastor: Do you promise to resist the power of sin and all that
destroys the unity of love within the human family?

Candidates: **I do.**

Pastor: Before asking that you become a new creation in Christ
Jesus, who alone can free you from its power, do you now
renounce all your past sin and its impact in your life?

Candidates: **I do.**

Pastor: Let us pray:

(The sponsors place their hands on the candidates shoulders.)

Fill us now, O God, with the saving power of Jesus.
Set us free from sin and death.
Give us a new awareness of being your children.
May these candidates keep your Word in their hearts,
so that they may know Christ,
who has come to seek and save that which was lost.
We give you thankful praise
because you sent your Son to be our Savior.
May your Word change their lives
that they may become a living witness
to your goodness and mercy.
Free them from all that holds them back
that they may discern your presence
always and everywhere in the world,
at work to heal and restore us to you.
We ask this through Christ our Lord.
Amen.

Pastor: Today this community, in the name of Christ, calls you to proceed in your journey to Christian baptism at Easter. You have already heard the call of Christ, and you have renounced evil. I now ask you:

Do you wish to enter fully into the fellowship of Christ through baptism?

Candidates: **I do.**

Pastor: Then I will ask you to offer your names for enrollment.

(The candidates first state their names and then write them in The Book of Enrollment. This book should be attractively decorated. When all are finished, the pastor continues naming all the candidates.)

Name, I now declare that you are a member of the elect, chosen by God, who is always faithful. Continue your journey, walking in love, so that you will meet Christ and receive the Spirit in the waters of baptism and with fire.

(To the sponsors:)

I ask you to continue with these friends in their time of spiritual growth, continue to sustain them by your prayer, your love, and your example, and aid them in their preparations for Christian baptism. Let us pray:

Holy God, you desire that all humanity
be made one in Christ.
We pray for your blessing on all your children.
Be with these friends who desire to join us in fellowship.
May we all become children of your promise
and rejoice in the life and grace you offer.
We ask this through Christ our Lord.

(To the candidates:)

My dear friends, today you have begun another stage of your journey toward the joy of life in the peace of God. Go now and may the peace of Christ be always with you. Amen.

Candidates: **Amen.**

SECOND SUNDAY IN LENT OR ADVENT: PRESENTATION OF A BIBLE

In the Advent version of this program, the Bible may be presented during the enrollment on the first Sunday in Advent.

Pastor: Again today, we ask candidates for baptism to come forward. My friends, this morning we wish to present you with a Bible. As you continue your preparation, may you hear the good news of God's love. Take this message to your hearts and joyfully share it with others.

Do you understand that as you receive this Bible, you are receiving the story of God's powerful and sustaining Word, and the good news of Jesus Christ?

Candidates: **I do.**

Pastor: Do you understand that this book speaks of God's love so that you may know the love of God and share this love with others?

Candidates: **I do.**

Pastor: Do you promise to hold God's Word in your heart and try to follow Jesus.

Candidate: **I do.**

Pastor: *(to the whole congregation)*

Now I turn to you, the people of God. Our friends have promised to be faithful to God's Word revealed in the Bible. Do you promise to be a faithful witness for them of the love of God and love of our neighbor that the Word of God celebrates?

Do you promise to encourage and support these candidates so that by your example of faithfulness, they will grow in faith, hope, and love?

All: **We do.**

Pastor: Let us pray for our friends assembled here, that God may set them free from sin and from all that separates them from God.

Holy God, we present to your care our brothers and sisters. (*See Prayer #1 for the First Sunday in Lent.*)

THIRD SUNDAY IN LENT OR SECOND SUNDAY IN ADVENT: CLEANSING

Scripture Reading
> Gospel: John 4:7–14

Pastor (to candidates): You have faithfully continued on your journey with Christ to the fullness of life in Christian baptism. Today the gospel calls upon us to be aware of our sin, so that we, like the woman of Samaria, can turn to Christ, the source of living water. This water will purify you and make you whole.

(To the whole congregation:) Let us pray in silence for our friends, that God's grace may come alive in them like streams of living water. May they never thirst again.

The congregation prays in silence. When silence is used in worship, enough time needs to be allowed for the silence to penetrate the congregation. A good rule of thumb is to pause for 10-15 seconds between each prayer.

Pastor: May they come to Christ, the living water and source of all life and holiness. O God of love,

All: **Hear our prayer.**

Pastor: May they discard everything in their lives that is opposed to Christ. O God of love,

All: **Hear our prayer.**

Pastor: May the Holy Spirit enable them to discern the way of faithful discipleship. O God of love,

All: **Hear our prayer.**

Pastor: Gracious God, you showed your presence
to the woman at the well,
and she ran out and proclaimed your good news.
May these candidates know your saving love,
your deliverance from all evil,
and your way of salvation so that they, too,
may worship you in spirit and in truth.
We pray this in the name of Jesus.
Amen.

Go now, and may the peace of Christ be always with you.

Candidates: **Amen.**

FOURTH SUNDAY IN LENT OR THIRD SUNDAY IN ADVENT: ILLUMINATION

Scripture Reading
John 9:1–11

Pastor: You have chosen to walk as children of light and to live a life of discipleship with Jesus Christ. Again, we pray that the grace of Christ will be active in your life as you prepare for Christian baptism. Today we pray that you will receive that light of Christ, so that you will never walk in darkness.

After a period of silence, the pastor continues with the prayers of intercession.

May God shine the light of love in our darkness.
Let us pray to the Lord.

All: **Lord, hear our prayer.**

Pastor: Gently lead these candidates to Christ, the light of the world. O God of love,

All: **Hear our prayer.**

Pastor: May the compassion of Christ heal you, and free you from all corruption. O God of love,

All: **Hear our prayer.**

Pastor: God of unfailing light, by the power of the cross of Jesus Christ you have dispelled all darkness. Enable these candidates to walk from death to new life in you.

We ask this through Christ, the light of the world.

All: **Amen.**

Pastor: Now we touch our candidates' ears and mouths, asking that they be opened to hear and proclaim the Word of God.

"Ephpheta": that is, to be opened, that you may hear the Word and confess it in faith, to the praise and glory of God.

Go now, and may the peace of Christ be always with you.

Candidates: **Amen.**

FIFTH SUNDAY IN LENT OR FOURTH SUNDAY IN ADVENT: SPIRITUAL RENEWAL

Scripture Reading
John 11:32–44

Pastor: God has chosen you to share in the death and resurrection of Jesus Christ. As the time for your baptism draws near, we will again pray for you that the same power that raised Christ from the dead will be active in you, so that you will be dead to sin and alive for God in Christ Jesus.

After a period of silence, the pastor continues:

Free them, O Lord from all pride so that their lives may give glory to God. O God of love,

All: **Hear our prayer.**

Pastor: Set them free from all selfishness so that they may live for others and follow the model of Christ who lived for others. O God of love,

All: **Hear our prayer.**

Pastor: Set them free from thoughts and feelings that are contrary to the love and compassion of Christ. O God of love,

All: **Hear our prayer.**

Pastor: Lord Jesus, you raised Lazarus from the dead,
to show that we might have more abundant life.
Free us from the ways of death
and enable us to choose your life-giving spirit.
Protect those you have chosen for baptism
and empower them with the glory of your resurrection.
Place all your people under the shelter of your wings,
that we might journey to life with God
with glad and joyful hearts.

All: **Amen.**

Pastor: Now we present you with a copy of the Lord's Prayer that you may be filled with the spirit of Jesus who prayed "Abba." When you pray to God, may this same Spirit fill you with faith, hope, and love.

Name, I present you with the Lord's Prayer. Through it, may you always know the love of God.

Now let us pray together the prayer that Jesus taught us. **Our Father....**

Go now and may the peace of Christ be always with you.

All: **Amen.**

STAGE THREE:
INCORPORATION INTO CHRIST

PALM SUNDAY OR SUNDAY AFTER CHRISTMAS

Pastor: This morning I offer you the great invitation to come forward and commit your lives to discipleship with Jesus Christ. We have traveled with you during your time of preparation and now we invite you to come forward to respond to the ancient profession of faith of the Christian community.

Name, do you, with Christians of every time and place, confess that Jesus is the Christ, the Son of the living God?

Candidate: **I do.**

Pastor (laying hands on the candidate and inviting the sponsors to place their hands on the candidate's shoulder):

May God bless you, *Name*, and keep you always in love. Amen.

(When all have made their confessions of faith.)

Pastor: Let us pray:

Holy God, with great joy and thanksgiving we accept these, your daughters and sons into a community of faith with you. Continue to send your love to them. By your Spirit, mold them into the image of your Son, Jesus.

May the abundant life you promised us in Jesus Christ be theirs. Amen.

PART THREE

Essays

CHILDREN AND CHRISTIAN BAPTISM

Ecumenical discussion of recent decades has stressed that baptism, at whatever age it is administered, should be placed within a context of Christian nurture that includes a) the growth of children within a supportive, instructing Christian community, b) a personal decision of faith expressed through public confession at an appropriate age, and c) periodic renewal of one's baptism and the life of discipleship toward which it points. Recognition of this context, in addition to closing the theological gap between infant baptism and believers' baptism, has raised important questions regarding the place of children in Christian community. If baptism means (among other things) incorporation into the body of Christ, is there any justification for excluding baptized children from various rituals or other activities of the church? In what sense is a child who has been dedicated really a part of the community of faith? How seriously has the church taken its responsibility to nurture children, baptized or not, toward confession and commitment? The purpose of this essay is to expand and clarify such questions by focusing on an issue of considerable concern to many contemporary Disciples—namely, the participation of children in the Lord's Supper.

There are parts of the universal church (e.g., the Orthodox churches) in which it is normal practice for baptized children, including infants, to receive the bread and wine of the Lord's Supper. In contrast, other parts of the church, including churches that baptize infants, have withheld communion until children reach some specified age. Two overlapping, but distinguishable, arguments are given for this practice: a) Churches that baptize infants have often contended that young children are unable to appreciate the meaning of communion, to approach it with proper awe, or to prepare for it through repentant self-examination. In these traditions, first communion has traditionally followed confirmation with its period of systematic instruction in the faith; b) churches that practice believers' baptism generally insist that the Lord's Supper be reserved until a person has become a member of the body of Christ through public confession of faith and baptism. These traditions have also usually agreed with the first group that children, until they reach the age of discretion, are not prepared to understand the significance of this meal and its relationship to Christian faith and discipleship.

In recent years, however, many churches that baptize infants have begun to rethink their traditional reluctance to admit children to the Lord's Table. The arguments given for this change, while not entirely applicable, may still prove valuable within a believers' baptism context.

First, educational and psychological studies over the past generation have led to a new appreciation for the ways children experience and understand the world. We now realize that children can and do have a sense of sin, a comprehension of God's gift of forgiveness and new life, and a love of Jesus Christ. What they do not have is the cognitive understanding of these realities characteristic of adulthood; but to require such understanding, churches now contend, may be to fence the Lord's Table on the basis of a far-too-narrow standard (one that would also exclude the mentally disabled and many of the elderly). In fact, if intellectual understanding is the criterion for participation in the Lord's Supper, people of all ages may feel unprepared to commune.

What recent studies show is that people know and learn in different ways at different stages of their lives. Children learn affectively, that is through experience. Attitudes and feelings are shaped, for example, by their encounters with Christian symbols and by their participation in the activities of the community. Churches are increasingly willing to encourage children's participation in the symbols and actions of the Lord's Supper (insisting only on an elementary grasp of the central affirmations of Christian faith), offering rational explanations of the experience at a later age.

Second, the point just made reflects changes in society that have freed children from traditional patterns of subservience by acknowledging that they are not simply "little adults" but persons with their own gifts and needs. Churches are beginning to recognize, however, that the special value and dignity of childhood are also affirmed in scripture. New attention is being paid to Jesus' command that the disciples not hinder children from coming to him (Matthew 19:13–14, Mark 10:14, Luke 18:16), to his pronouncement that unless we "change and become like children" we will not enter the kingdom of heaven (Matthew 18:3), and to his rejoicing that God has hidden from "the wise and the intelligent" what has been revealed to babes (Matthew 11:25, Luke 10:21). Other New Testament passages do suggest that children are to grow in understanding and maturity (e.g., 1 Corinthians 13:11), but, from the biblical perspective, adults have much to learn from the model of childhood. When children come to the Lord's Supper with trust and eagerness, when they come without any sense of having "earned" God's grace, they may well reveal new dimensions of faith to other participants.

The passage most often cited in opposition to children's communion is 1 Corinthians 11:27 ff: A person must not eat or drink "in an unworthy manner" but must come to the meal after self-examination. It is clear from the context, however, that Paul is not here dealing with the question of children's admission to the Lord's Supper. His concern is with the way the rich persons used the celebrations in Corinth as a private feast from which other members of the community were excluded. Such persons, says the apostle, eat and drink judgment upon themselves by the way they violate the oneness of Christ's body. The specific issue of admitting children to the meal (or, for that matter, the more general issue of whether baptism is a necessary prerequisite to participation in the Eucharist) is never directly addressed in the New Testament.

Third, new understandings of the sacraments, emerging from ecumenical dialogue, have also contributed to the change we have been discussing. Protestant churches, for example, are now affirming more clearly than they often have in the past that, through the Holy Spirit, God is actively present in the celebration of communion. This meal, in other words, is not merely an exercise in pious recollection (dependent upon *our* ability to remember and understand) but a response to the present grace of God that nourishes and guides us in all the stages of life.

We have already noted the deepened appreciation of baptism as part of a lifelong process of growth and nurture. Confirmation, understood in this perspective, is not the "completion" of baptism but a sign of one's growing incorporation into the life of Christ through the work of God's Spirit. Children are thus seen as full partners in the community's life prior to the time that they receive systematic instruction in the faith and confess it publicly.

Fourth, we return to the heart of the issue. Since a person becomes a full member of Christ's church through baptism, there is really no theological basis for excluding some members from the community's common meal on the basis of age. God gathers persons of all cultures, races, classes, and ages into a new community whose most profound symbol of unity is the one loaf of the Lord's Table (1 Corinthians 10:17). The admission of baptized children to the Eucharist is, thus, increasingly viewed as a sign of the church's essential inclusivity.

This, of course, is where the Disciples experience differs from that of our Methodist or Presbyterian or United Church of Christ neighbors. The universal church has generally held that baptism, at whatever age, is a necessary precondition for receiving the Lord's Supper. This meal is the church's "feast of joy," and non-baptized children, according to the above stated definition, are not members of the church. It is those who have "put on Christ" through baptism who participate in the body and blood of Christ through the Eucharist.

But the issue is not as simple as this. For one thing, recent theological discussion has emphasized the eschatological character of the Lord's Supper—the way it represents, in other words, the coming reign of God throughout creation. This has led some Christian scholars (e.g., Jürgen Moltmann and Geoffrey Wainwright) to conclude that the meal should not be conceived as a "churchly event" at all. Because Christ died for the reconciliation of the world, the world is invited to this vivid symbol and celebration of what it is to become. From this perspective, Christ's table is open without condition to everyone.

For another, the experience of many Disciples parents convinces them that there is something incorrect about speaking of the unbaptized children of believing, participating parents as outside the Christian community. The understanding of Christian life as a communal process of nurture and growth from cradle to grave (mentioned above) surely applies to traditions that dedicate infants while reserving baptism for an age of personal confession and commitment. The community has dedicated itself to raising the children of its members in a Christian context toward the day when the children will, we pray, make individual decisions of faith and be baptized. Already they are, by way of anticipation, part of the family.

Behind the conviction growing out of our experience as parents is the broader issue of the nature of the church. The tradition of believers' baptism underscores that membership in the body of Christ involves decision, risk, commitment. While saying this, however, we also affirm that the church is not simply a collection of confessing individuals. It is a community, a spirit-filled whole greater than the sum of its parts, that, as a body, nurtures its children and cares for its weak or disabled members. The greater this sense of nurturing community, the more pressure there will be to include children in the celebration of the church.

Finally, since the majority of Disciples congregations now practice open membership, many of our communities include young children who were baptized in other traditions. We have seen that there are strong arguments in favor of inviting these persons to the table; indeed, given the new thinking about children and communion, they may have been regular communicants in their former churches. But that presents us with the uncomfortable prospect of serving the bread and the cup to some children (i.e., those already baptized) while withholding it from others (i.e., those not yet baptized).

The question is more difficult for Disciples than for other churches that practice believers' baptism because of our insistence (also part of the growing ecumenical understanding) that the Lord's Supper is the climax of the church's worship and should, therefore, be celebrated as the normal service of a congregation's worship. There is no doubt that children in Disciples congregations feel left out as the trays are passed over them each Sunday.

There are no easy answers to the questions raised at the beginning of this essay. Four conclusions, however, can be offered.

1. Disciples need to work more intentionally and effectively to include children in the life of the church and to prepare in them the ground for a mature faith. One way to include children is for congregations to conduct worship services that are deliberately designed to include persons of all ages. Another way is suggested by the practice in some traditions of having children who do not yet take communion to come forward with their parents and receive a blessing from the celebrant. This is harder to envision in a church where communion is served by deacons to people seated in pews. Still, it is possible and appropriate for the invitation to the table to acknowledge the community's children and to pray that God will bless those who have been placed in the community's care.

2. Many people are no longer convinced, on theological grounds, that unbaptized children should be excluded from the table. Yet, the decision to include children is *not* one that should be left simply to the discretion of individual families. For one thing, this approach is guaranteed to produce a diversity of practice that will be more confusing then enriching. For another, since most Christian traditions regard baptism as the prerequisite to communion, widespread deviation from that pattern could have serious ecumenical consequences that need to be recognized. It is important, therefore, that Disciples find ways to think through this issue *as a church* in order to offer guidance for congregations and families as they make decisions about children in relation to baptism.

The Commission on Theology and other theologians and liturgical scholars would perform an important service to our church by taking the lead in this process.

3. Congregations can (and do) participate in this process of study and exploration of new possibilities. Since the issues involved reach to the center of the church's life and its convictions about salvation, the eldership of a congregation is the place where discussions should be lodged. Certainly the pastor and others on the pastoral team should be involved. Parents and children are appropriate participants in the conversation. Because the issues necessarily involve people in other church traditions, a congregation's study should include conversations with representative groups in other churches with whom Disciples are in relationship.

As a congregation's study moves forward, families need to be kept abreast of recommendations and policies. The people who conduct the Lord's Supper and administer the communion elements need to be helped to understand policies, and they should be instructed in what they should do. These efforts to instruct and nurture people are especially important in congregations that establish policies that permit unbaptized children to receive communion. In congregations that do not establish such policies, it still is important to instruct families, elders, and deacons. Everyone needs to be helped to participate in the communion service to whatever extent that policy provides. When policy withholds the privilege, there is strong reason to provide both interpretation of the policy and reassurance of those whom the policy cannot admit.

4. What is implied above needs to be stated explicitly. Whatever the decisions reached about unbaptized children and communion, Disciples can strengthen their programs of instruction in the meaning of the Lord's Supper. This instruction should help all worshipers as they hear the word, give offerings, sing communion hymns, and listen to the prayers. Worshipers need to be taught ways of personal prayerfulness that can help them grasp the import of the service and be grasped by the dramatic actions around the table. In congregations that give this kind of attention to instruction and nurture, admission to the table will take on new power for all who hear and respond to Christ's generous invitation to take and eat in remembrance of him.

EASTER AND THE CELEBRATION
OF BAPTISM

The celebration of baptism has long been associated with the Easter season. This close connection is being confirmed in many churches by the modern revival of an ancient service—the Easter Vigil. (For a description of the Easter Vigil and a full text for the service, see pages 67-88.) The purpose of this essay is to describe the historical linkage of Easter and baptism and to recommend that Disciples congregations celebrate the Easter Vigil.

Easter

Easter is the source and climax of Christian worship. All time, for the Christian, is understood and charted from this moment that celebrates our salvation history. Christ died for us and was raised from the dead. In his death and resurrection we live. It is a moment to be anticipated, exalted in, remembered.

Easter cannot be repeated. It stands as a unique moment in God's redemptive drama. Yet, it guides and empowers the church's ongoing story of salvation history. Annually the church recites and re-enacts Jesus' passion and resurrection. Weekly, smaller Easters are celebrated when the church assembles on Sunday, the day of resurrection, to hear the word and break the bread and to anticipate the fuller feast in heaven. Easter is a glory-filled moment fully given in first-century Palestine and yet given again in the continuing narrative of God's bringing salvation to a waiting, hoping, remembering, celebrating people.

The Easter story celebrates Jesus of Nazareth, the anointed of God. Jesus lived as an itinerant teacher and preacher who came announcing a message of justice and shalom. God's time of justice and shalom has finally begun. The new reign of God is here, now. This Jesus and the message of the Kingdom were so closely identified with each other that they became as one. Those threatened by the message

131

attacked the messenger. This person of justice and shalom who inaugurated God's reign was victimized by an unimaginably unjust and violent death. He was crucified. And the message and messenger of justice and shalom were silenced.

But violence and injustice did not have the final word. There was a wonderful "gettin' up mornin'!" Jesus Christ arose! The reign of God's justice and shalom has truly come and lives on after the awful testing! And the people of God have anticipated and remembered and celebrated yearly and weekly ever since! Easter is the source and climax of Christian worship.

The earliest celebrations of Easter were associated with the Jewish celebration of passover, pascha. The night of Jesus' betrayal and the day of his death occurred when Jerusalem was filled with the faithful celebrating pascha. Paul, in an early description of Easter, clearly links Passover and Easter.

> For our paschal lamb, Christ, has been sacrificed. Therefore, let us celebrate the festival, not with the old yeast, the yeast of malice and evil, but with the unleavened bread of sincerity and truth .
>
> 1 Corinthians 5:6b–8

Marion Hatchett, in his commentary on *The Book of Common Prayer*, helps draw the connections between Passover and Easter.

> The Jewish Passover commemorated the slaying of the firstborn, the exodus from Egypt, and the entry into the Promised Land. Jesus Christ was the fulfillment of the old feast for the early church. In almost every language, except English, the same word is used for the Jewish Passover and the Christian Easter—pascha. Some authors find the feast, reinterpreted, celebrated within New Testament times and associated with baptism, with the imagery of the Passover recalled—Exodus, the Passover, and the entrance into the Promised Land.[30]

Easter Baptism

Easter is the time the early church chose to baptize those who had been in preparation for entering the church. The choice clearly established the link between Passover and baptism. In baptism, the faithful pass from death to life as they remember and celebrate their Hebrew ancestors' passing from slavery to freedom. In Easter-baptism, the faithful pass from death to life as they celebrate Jesus' passing from death to life. It is the occasion of regeneration.

> What time is more appropriate for baptism than this day of the Pasch? It is the memorial day of the resurrection. Baptism implants in us the Seed of Resurrection. Let us then receive the grace of the day of Resurrection on the day of the resurrection.[31]

St. Basil's declaration on baptism, given in the fourth century, affirms Easter as the occasion for baptism. On that day, Christ's passion and resurrection are enriched with the memory of the Hebrew people's experience of passing from death to life, from slavery to freedom, from life as drudgery to life as promise. Even today those to be baptized on Easter enter the water with the baptized of the ancient church and with them remember God's ongoing acts of liberation. Ancient Christians and today's new Christians are joint heirs of Christ's promise of resurrection.

Baptism was received after instruction and preparation. The Acts of the Apostles help us recall Philip teaching the Ethiopian, beginning with the book of Isaiah, and then teaching him about Jesus Christ. Then Philip baptized the man (Acts 8:26–40). The letter to the Hebrews hints at what may be the church's earliest practices of preparation for baptism.

> Therefore let us go on toward perfection, leaving behind the basic teaching about Christ, and not laying again the foundation: repentance from dead works and faith toward God, instruction about baptisms, laying on of hands, resurrection of the dead, and eternal judgment. And we will do this, if God permits. For it is impossible to restore again to repentance those who have once been enlightened, and have tasted the heavenly gift, and have shared in the Holy Spirit, and have tasted the goodness of the word of God and the powers of the age to come....
> Hebrews 6:1–5

Justin Martyr, in about A.D.150, spoke of teaching those preparing for baptism to fast and pray. Note also that the church enters these same disciplines with them.

> Those who are convinced and believe what we say and teach is the truth, and pledge themselves to be able to live accordingly, are taught in prayer and fasting to ask God to forgive their past sins, while we pray and fast with them.

Then we lead them to a place where there is water, and they are regenerated in the same manner in which we ourselves were regenerated.[32]

Our most detailed account of baptism, including the preparation for baptism, comes from Hippolytus in about A.D. 200. He describes the practices of the church of Rome. Corroborative evidence suggests that these practices were widely used in the ancient church, but with minor local variations.

Hippolytus describes a thorough selection and preparation of the candidates for baptism.

They who are to be set apart for baptism shall be chosen after their lives have been examined: whether they have lived soberly, whether they have honoured the widows, whether they have visited the sick, whether they have been active in well-doing. When their sponsors have testified that they have done these things, then let them hear the Gospel...hands shall be laid upon them daily in exorcism and, as the day of their baptism draws near, the bishop himself shall exorcise (or, "exacts an oath from") each one of them that he may be personally assured of their purity.[33]

Hippolytus goes on to detail the preparation of the catechumens in the week of Christ's passion.

Then those who are set apart for baptism shall be instructed to bathe and free themselves from impurity and wash themselves on Thursday....

They who are to be baptized shall fast on Friday, and on Saturday the bishop shall assemble them and command them to kneel in prayer. And, laying his hand upon them, he shall exorcise all evil spirits to flee away and never to return; when he has done this, he shall breathe in their faces, seal their foreheads, ears and noses, and then raise them up. They shall spend all that night in vigil, listening to reading and instruction.[34]

At cockcrow they move from fast to festival. The water of baptism is blessed. Prayers are said over the oils of exorcism and thanksgiving. The rites begin.

With some imagination we can picture a gathering of a small group of persons to be baptized before a bishop and presbyter. Each person to be baptized faces west, into the darkness, and renounces Satan. "I renounce you, Satan, and all your service and all your works." Each is then anointed with the oil of exorcism.

Next, each one walks down into the water of the baptistry. Three times each is dramatically buried in the water. The presbyter asks, "Do you believe in God the Father Almighty?" "I believe," responds the convert. He or she is immersed the first time. "Do you believe in Christ Jesus, the Son of God?" "I believe." The convert is immersed the second time. "Do you believe in the Holy Spirit, in the Holy Church and in the resurrection of the flesh?" "I believe." Each convert is immersed a third time.

The newly baptized member comes up out of the water and is there greeted by the bishop, is dressed in a white robe (the baptism was done in the nude), and anointed with the oil of thanksgiving.

Now the group of newly baptized members is ready to join the gathered congregation. They are taken to the assembly where the bishop places hands on each convert and prays that the Spirit empower them to serve as God wills. Each person's forehead is touched, tracing the shape of the cross. They join with the congregation in the prayers of the people, the passing of the peace and the Eucharist. For this special communion, the newly baptized also receive water (an internal baptism) and milk and honey (the food of babies, the food of the Promised Land) as well as bread and wine.

Easter Vigil continued to be celebrated as the climactic service of the church's calendar until at least the fourth century. As late as the end of the fourth century, Easter Vigil occupied the entire night with no service celebrated on Easter Day.

Over the next several centuries regulations on fasting were relaxed. The Vigil was celebrated earlier and earlier. By the sixteenth century the rite had been reduced to lighting the Easter candle and carrying it to the altar in the broad daylight of Saturday morning! This was far from the liturgical experience of the third century when the Vigil was in the dark of Saturday night and the dawn of Sunday morning. Then the worshiper experienced the great antithesis between night and day, fasting and the eucharistic meal, mourning and festive joy. The liturgical experience allowed them to know the joy of moving from death to new life in Christ.

Easter Vigil as a central vivid moment in the life of the church was lost to the use of the church for much of the church's life.

Recovery of the Easter Vigil

The Easter Vigil is being recovered in our time. The recovery is promising. In time, Easter Vigil may even be restored to the centrality and significance that benefited the church of the third and fourth centuries.

The Roman Catholic Church began the recovery of Easter Vigil in 1951 when Pope Pius XII allowed, as an experiment, the Vigil to be celebrated in the night before Easter. It became general law in 1955. Now, in the Rites of Christian Initiation of Adults, Easter Vigil is the climactic service of the year in many parishes.

More recently, other churches have published services of Easter Vigil. They appear in the *Lutheran Book of Worship*, 1978, *The Book of Common Prayer*, 1979, *The Book of Worship/United Church of Christ*, 1986, and *Handbook of the Christian Year*, 1986 (United Methodist).

Easter Vigil is a rite particularly commendable to Disciples congregations. It has integrity with our founders' vision. It is ecumenical. It lifts up baptism and preparation for baptism. It is apostolic.

Alexander Campbell did not encourage the special celebration of the resurrection on Easter Sunday. There is not a single notation for Easter in the index of the *"Millennial Harbinger,"* the journal he published for 36 years. For Campbell, every Sunday was Easter! Yet, it can be argued that Easter Vigil expresses the faith in a way deeply valued by Disciples.

First, the Vigil is an effective way of expressing a central theme in the Disciples tradition. Christ's cross and resurrection are paramount in understanding God's action of regenerating humanity. The death, burial, and resurrection of Jesus Christ fill the minds and hearts of the believers whenever they see anyone enter the water of baptism. They touch the "affections" of the believers every week when bread is broken. Those motifs are motifs of pascha, Easter.

Easter Vigil is a way to give liturgical expression to Campbell's and the Disciples' view of the central elements in the drama of salvation. While Campbell did not speak of Easter Vigil, he did speak of rites essential in the vivid portrayal of redemption. Note Campbell's view of baptism as regenerative, which is in keeping with the paschal themes in Easter Vigil.

> Indeed we may truthfully say, that the meaning, or intent of the positive institutions of the gospel is to develope (sic) and to perpetuate this redemption. They are, one and all, monumental institutions.

> Baptism, is indeed, monumental of his death, burial and resurrection. Hence they who are "dead to sin, are buried with him in Baptism; rise with him, from the symbolic grave to walk in a new life."

The Lord's day celebrates his triumphant resurrection, the greatest event that ever was inscribed on the records of time.

The Lord's Supper perpetuates the memory of his sacrificial death; and is, therefore, the weekly Christian feast of his blood-ransomed friends. These three positive institutions, in their proper conception, comprehend the rudimental elements of the whole remedial system. They are monumental in the highest conception of the term, and comprehend all that is evangelically indicated in that sublime and beatific term, *redemption*. This is, in all truth, a word of the most soul-stirring eloquence, indicative of all that can beautify, beatify, and glorify man forever.[35]

Second, the Vigil is particularly commendable to Disciples because it can demonstrate their participation in the developing ecumenical consensus. Thomas and Alexander Campbell called for the church to both pursue and recognize its oneness. "The church is essentially, intentionally and constitutionally one."

The heart of the Disciples passion and plea has been ecumenism. Disciples have dreamed and at times even sacrificed to move the church of God to unity in Christ and the mutual enrichment of the churches as each shares from its unique heritage. Disciples are open to receive. Disciples celebrate theological convergence and shared worship and mission.

Along with the pursuit of unity has been the recognition of unity when and where it already exists. Alexander Campbell recognized an existing ecumenism in the consensus of Protestantism in observing three institutions: baptism, the Lord's Day, and the Lord's Supper.

By almost, if not altogether common consent of all Protestantdom, there are, at least, three christian positive commemorative institutions. These are Christian Baptism, the Lord's Day, and the Lord's Supper.[36]

Today's Disciples can both recognize and pursue unity in the ecumenical convergence around such rites as Easter Vigil. A mark of unity in Western Christianity is the annual shared day of celebrating Christ's resurrection. Disciples, with many churches of the West, have held Easter to be the primary event of Christian celebration.

In the Easter Vigil this Christocentric church, the Christian Church (Disciples of Christ), receives from the larger church a fuller way to celebrate our waiting for and entering into Christ's resurrection. It is one more sign that Disciples believe God wills the church to be one and, in God's time, that the church will be one. In the meantime,

Christians welcome those moments of waiting and celebrating together. Easter Vigil is commendable to Disciples as an ecumenical church.

Third, Easter Vigil is commendable to Disciples because it enriches the congregation's participation in the drama of salvation. The ancient Easter Vigil offers an excellent opportunity to expand and enrich the baptism event. Suggested fuller rites of baptism at Easter Vigil are offered in the liturgical material of this book. A congregation could implement the training of sponsors. One of the commitments of sponsors would be an intense day of intercession on the Saturday of the Vigil. Persons in preparation for baptism and their sponsors would have limited activity and socialization. In solitude and silence they would spend much of the day in prayer. In keeping with the ancient preparation for baptism, sponsors and candidates could choose to fast for the day and break the fast with a first meal after the service of Easter Vigil.

Disciples have taught and encouraged the practice of believers' baptism. Through exposure to the Christian gospel, one responds in joyful obedience by being buried in the water of baptism and raised to new life. Easter Vigil offers encouragement from the ancient church both in the preparation of persons for baptism and the practice of immersion as the form of baptism.

Fourth, Easter Vigil is commendable to Disciples because of its apostolic roots. It connects Disciples practice to the baptismal practice of the early church. Disciples strategy for guiding the practices of the church has been to turn prayerfully to scripture. "Restorationism," over time, has proven to be a naive and flawed strategy. Yet our rejection of the restoration principle does not mean that the church is to be indifferent to grounding the life and faith of the church in scripture. Disciples today are learning again how to take scripture seriously.

The early writings of the church describe serious preparation of candidates for baptism, with "instruction about baptisms, laying on of hands, resurrection of the dead, and eternal judgment" (Hebrews 6:2). We do not have detailed descriptions of services of baptism from the earliest days of the church. Yet, we can be guided by services described for us that occurred within one hundred years of the writing of the Christian scriptures.

Easter Vigil is a commendable occasion for baptizing new members. It is not to replace our common sense guideline of baptizing whenever anyone is ready to come into the new life of Christ's people. Easter Vigil is a desirable alternate time for baptism. As the church becomes more experienced in worshiping at Easter Vigil, baptism in that service may even grow from a desirable alternate time to the church's normative occasion for baptism.

Fasting, vigil, the assembling of the faithful for significant rites of baptism on Easter eve may even become the climactic way for Disciples to celebrate the ancient yet modern story of new life in Jesus Christ.

TRADITION, AUTHORITY, AND THE BAPTISMAL FORMULA

Into what name are we to baptize? Are we to continue the practice of the church since the first century and baptize "in the name of the Father and of the Son and of the Holy Spirit"? (See Matthew 28:19.) Or are we to adopt another name for the ordinance at the entrance to the Christian life? This question about the baptismal formula brings into conflict two ideas that stand at the center of theological discussion in our time. The first is that baptism is the rite that establishes the Christian identity of each one who is baptized. Thus, the name of God used in baptism must be the name that the church universal gives to us. The other element is the conviction that the language we use to talk to God and about God—even the language given us by the church through the ages—must transcend the predominantly masculine language forms that currently are in use. Thus a formula like Father, Son, and Holy Spirit needs to be reconsidered and other metaphorical titles for the triune God should be used as possibilities.

The Tradition: Baptism in the Threefold Name of God

The long-standing consensus of church practice is clear. In the earliest period, converts came from Judaism. They already believed in God. What was distinctive about their new religious condition was their belief in Jesus as the Messiah. Thus they were directed to be baptized "in the name of Jesus Christ so that your sins may be forgiven" (Acts 2:38). Soon thereafter, converts from non-Jewish sources came to be baptized and the name used at baptism was enlarged. The baptismal name stated in Matthew 28:19 is based on this later development: "in the name of the Father and of the Son and of the Holy Spirit."

The early generations of the church's life were dominated by several struggles in which this threefold name of God was central. One struggle developed as Christians tried to understand how their

140

experience of "God in Christ" was distinct from the God experienced by Jews, Greeks, Romans, and Orientals in the Roman Empire. The second struggle came as Christians faced persecution in their effort to remain true to their Christian faith. The identifying sign, the brand, the basic mark of Christian identity was this faith in God whose true identity and revelation could be described in the threefold name of Father, Son, and Holy Spirit. The one place where all of the theological and ethical issues came to focus was baptism, for here people risked everything they were and could ever hope to be. They severed their ties with the beliefs, values, and doctrines of the dominant culture and committed themselves to Christ and the Christian life of witness, service, and suffering. Therefore, at the high point of the baptismal liturgy, when candidates were brought powerfully to the waters of regeneration, forgiveness, and cleansing, the church invoked the name over which the most ink and blood had been shed: Father, Son, and Holy Spirit.

In East and West, in Protestant and Catholic churches alike, this practice has been maintained for virtually the entire history of the Christian faith. Even though churches have differed greatly over the age when baptism should take place, the way that water is to be used, and the theological meaning of this rite, they have been agreed that baptism uses water, and that it is "in the name of the Father and of the Son and of the Holy Spirit." Any effort to talk about "one baptism" (see Ephesians 4:5) has been based on this twofold minimum of sacramental element and defining formula.

The importance of this consensus has increased since mid-century. During this 40-year period, the churches have moved significantly to overcome the fractured character of the one church of Christ, the church that we know by faith to be one even though we experience it as divided. The fact that we have all been baptized in the "one baptism" has become the foundation for much of the theological discussion and movement toward reconciliation. An especially clear example is the importance of the mutual recognition of members by the churches in the Consultation on Church Union. A few years ago the churches in the Consultation developed a statement which affirms that all baptized members of each church are fully members of the one church of Christ. The implications of this assertion are that church membership transcends denominational membership, that the free exchange of membership is not only possible but necessary because we are one in Christ, that there should not be impediments to this possibility of transfer from one communion to another.

The next step is now being taken, the assertion that because there is one baptism there also is one ministry. The current development within COCU is the effort to create a covenantal relationship based on this belief that our common baptism makes us one. The churches in the Consultation are making ready to declare publicly that one another's churches are true churches of Christ, that one another's ministries are true ministries of Christ, that one another's sacraments are true sacraments of Christ. A series of church decisions and public liturgies are being developed that will bring about a reconciliation of pastors with ordaining responsibilities so that henceforth all ordinations within the churches of the Consultation will be perceived as equally valid and efficacious by all of the churches of the Consultation. One of the elements in the covenant will be the pledge that henceforth in all of the churches we will celebrate the basic acts of worship with liturgies that are mutually acceptable.

Of course, many inter-church relations take place outside of the context of the Consultation on Church Union. Relations with the Lutheran, Catholic, and Orthodox branches of the church will require even more than within American protestantism that the foundation of inter-church relations and transfer of members will be baptism in water in the name of the Father, Son, and Holy Spirit. Relations with evangelical Christianity are more ambiguous. There is the possibility that some will insist upon the biblical language of "into the name of Jesus." With respect to baptism, these churches are traditionalist in practice, they are not much persuaded by feminist or inclusivist ideas.

Toward a New Consensus: God Beyond Gender

Recent theological discussions have dealt seriously with the relationship between theological language about God and the actuality of God. Of course, this discussion has always taken place, but a new dimension has arisen in recent decades. When we take seriously the claim that the titles for God are metaphors, we must acknowledge that all of the titles are true and also misleading, that they help us perceive the God of experience and faith, but that they also obscure this same God. Even so important a title as Father, if it is a metaphor, has these two features of truth and untruth.

Yet the religious language of Christian prayer and the more technical language of theology have made much use of this one title. Jesus gave us the example, and later doctrinal controversies helped to establish the practice. This title has a prominent place in the two ancient ecumenical creeds. It has also become deeply ingrained in the liturgy, especially in the prayer cycles of the daily office. Interestingly, Father is much less used in the brief prayers of the eucharistic liturgy, although it has always been prominent in the eucharistic prayer.

The danger that arises when one title becomes so dominant is that it takes on an exclusivist character. It comes to be treated as though it were absolutely true in a way that no other title can be. This fixation upon one term can be considered idolatry and therefore is to be avoided.

This problem is intensified when the title in question has negative social implications. The history of male domination in personal, family, cultural, and political life is clear. The oppressiveness of this domination can also be attested. It can be demonstrated that there is a reciprocal relationship between the use of male metaphors for the divine and this cultural fact of male domination in society. The elevation of male and the simultaneous lowering of female categories give society an unhealthy character. Furthermore, it is destructive of health both for men and women. It gives men an unreal sense of their power and worth. It undermines women's sense of worth and maims their readiness to exercise their powers in personal and social life.

Thus the discussion about God and gender is a discussion about truth: Who is God? How can our human language talk about God? Who are we as men? Who are we as women? How can language drawn from human life be used to talk about relations with the divine?

These questions are altering radically the language of praise and petition. In time, they will alter the language of formal theological discourse. Finally, there will be significant changes in the theological formulas that the churches use to protect their self-identity. These changes come with difficulty. We are not sure how to distinguish between the many names and nicknames for God. Some work better in prayers than others do. Theological discourse requires comprehensiveness, adequacy, and intelligibility. The process of thinking through the implications of changing the normal language about God is time consuming and laborious. It also is controversial. It moves forward unevenly, with some people moving out ahead of the consensus and others holding back. Progress comes with a seesawing motion.

With so much at stake in the discussion about God and gender, it is understandable that battles take place at the center of Christian identity. If we can transform the sacrament at the entrance to the Christian life, then it will become possible to deal with the issues at other points, too. Thus, the long-standing practice of baptizing with only one form of the naming of the trinitarian God needs to be challenged. Other forms of naming could be introduced, thus indicating that even Father, Son, and Holy Spirit is metaphorical and that the Christian understanding of God can be expressed in other language, too.

The desirability of changing the divine name in baptism can be seen in two other ways. When baptizing pastors find that their own personal identity and theological convictions are compromised by the exclusive use of the one formula, then the need to change the formula can be argued. Furthermore, the same situation will arise with some of the people who come to be baptized. Their own sense of identity and theological conviction will be challenged if baptism must always be in the name of Father, Son, and Holy Spirit.

Pastoral Authority and Responsibility

What is developing is the classic struggle between an unmovable object and an irresistible force. The ecclesial tradition at this time is unyielding. Although the reasons vary widely, the one formula that most churches accept for baptism is the traditional baptism "in the name of the Father and of the Son and of the Holy Spirit." Representatives of some churches indicate that their church authorities are likely to adopt new disciplines for transfer of members if the classical language is replaced. Baptisms using other names for God, such as Creator, Redeemer, and Sustainer, would not be recognized.

The result would be that people baptized with these other formulas would be required to be rebaptized when they seek to transfer membership. Technically, they would not be rebaptized since the first action would not be recognized as baptism.

The issue for pastors can be stated this way: Do they act as representatives of the church or as self-governing professionals? A parallel situation is pastoral authority to perform weddings. Do pastors act as representatives of the church—and of the state—or do they act as persons who possess in their own right the power to conduct weddings and sign the legal papers? And whichever way these questions are answered, how much discretionary authority do ordained pastors have as they conduct public rites and ceremonies?

The answer that is implicit in this paper is that with respect to baptism, pastors represent the church not themselves. They have extensive discretionary power to determine when baptism may take place, the people who may be baptized, and the specific details of the baptismal liturgy. They do not have discretionary power to do away with water or to change the baptismal formula. They may choose not to baptize, if the churches' requirements violate conscience. But some of the churches are stating that their own identity and the identity of their members requires that the use of water in the name of Father, Son, and Holy Spirit are necessary components of the baptismal rite.

Is there anything that can be done to change this situation? Or to put the question more forcefully, how will the change ever take place if we yield at the point of the baptismal formula? If we give up the battle here, doesn't that mean that we have surrendered? Or that the battle at every other point is trivialized? These questions prompt the following observations.

First, the limitation of ritual freedom leads to the enlarging of liturgical responsibilities and the strengthening of the teaching office of pastors. The baptismal formula and water are currently fixed, but the text of the rest of the liturgy is not. In many churches pastors have considerable freedom in choosing scripture readings, hymns, and other parts of the liturgy. They frequently have the authority to develop the prayers, even the prayer over the water and the prayer for the people baptized. Here the liturgy may be much more expansive in the way that it uses language about God and humankind. Some pastors may even be persuaded to retain the traditional formula but to embellish it with a balancing metaphor. Most, however, will provide balancing materials elsewhere in the service.

Furthermore, pastors have the authority and responsibility to teach their people about God and about the limitations of all of our human discourse about God. The metaphorical character even of the classical trinitarian formula needs to be taught to the people of the churches. Most pastors are likely to find their skill and courage tried to the limits as they plunge into this aspect of the teaching office. With respect to many practices of the church, pastors have a difficult responsibility: to explain to people why the church requires what it does. The first scandal to stand in the way of membership is not the trinitarian formula but the fact of baptism itself—and this especially in churches that practice the ancient rite of immersion. Why should a self-respecting adult submit to that public rite when so many other initiatory processes could be devised? The teaching office is important.

Second, there are opportunities to discuss and debate these questions about God, church membership, and baptism where the results may gradually affect the councils of the church. It is not clear that the liturgical commissions of churches or the governing bodies of denominations can change the baptismal formula. Their authority may be great, but their powers are also very limited. In these circles, however, the possibility of ecclesial change is present. When pastors debate the questions of God language in these settings, they are risking themselves. The cogency of their thought, their ability to stand up under attack, their resiliency, their willingness to risk reprisal are all being tested. In these settings, intelligence, knowledge, persuasiveness, and persistence are required because pastors are talking with their peers and superiors.

In all of these discussions—with people coming to baptism and in the councils of the church—two loyalties must always be kept in close relations with each other. The one loyalty is to the truth as revealed in scripture, developed in the church's tradition and confirmed in the theological reflections of each new era. The other loyalty is to the current life of Christians in the church and in the world, a life that keeps changing and therefore never fits easily in prevailing patterns of doctrine and discipline. Every pastoral conversation, every instruction about baptism, every new celebration of baptismal rites and ceremonies is a new negotiation of these two loyalties. We do not yet know how this process of discussion and experimentation will be resolved. What we do know is that through it all the Holy Spirit works to bring people to faith and new life in Jesus Christ.

Notes

[1]Among the books that discuss this transformation in baptism are the following: *Baptism: Christ's Act in the Church*, by Lawrence Hull Stookey, Abingdon Press, 1982; *Baptismal Moments; Baptismal Meanings*, by Daniel B. Stevick, The Church Hymnal Corporation, 1987; *Made, Not Born: New Perspectives on Christian Initiation and the Catechumenate*, University of Notre Dame Press, 1976; *The Shape of Baptism: The Rite of Christian Initiation*, by Aidan Kavanaugh, Pueblo Publishing Company, 1978.

[2]William Robinson, *What Churches of Christ Stand For*. The Berean Press, 1946, p. 55.

[3]Quoted by Clark M. Williamson in *Baptism: Embodiment of the Gospel*. Christian Board of Publication, 1987, p. 38; from the Walker-Campbell Debate of 1822, p. 179.

[4]From *Holy Baptism and Services for the Renewal of Baptism: The Worship of God (Supplemental Liturgical Resource 2)*, p. 32. Copyright © 1985 Westminster Press. Used by permission of Westminster/John Knox Press.

[5]This service is respectfully dedicated to the members of Pleasant Union Christian Church (Disciples of Christ), Newton Grove, NC. The Blessing of the Waters was adapted from a eucharistic prayer, "Water," by Donald Gelpi, S.J. in *Bread Blessed and Broken: Eucharistic Prayers and Fraction Rites*, John P. Mossi, S.J. ed. Paulist Press, 1969, pp. 72-74. Copyright © 1974 by The Missionary Society of St. Paul the Apostle in the State of New York. Used by permission of Paulist Press.

[6]This service is revised from the liturgy published by the consultation on Church Union under the title *An Order for the Celebration of Holy Baptism* (Princeton, NJ, 1973), pp. 29-34.

[7]Sponsors are mature Christians who accompany people coming to baptism. Sponsors may be members of the family, elders of the congregation, members of the evangelism group, or friends in the congregation who encourage the candidates and indicate their readiness to help the newly baptized grow in the Christian faith and life. Ordinarily, two to four persons would act as sponsors for each one who comes to be baptized.

[8]Oil used for anointing is olive oil mixed with an aromatic oil such as oil of balsam. The pastor moistens the tip of his or her thumb and lightly rubs the forehead of the one baptized in the shape of a small cross.

[9]This service and commentary are revised from "A Word to the Church on Baptism: Report of the Commission on Theology, 1987," published as an appendix to *Baptism: Embodiment of the Gospel* by Clark M. Williamson. Christian Board of Publication 1987, pp. 55-60.

[10]The instruction and the first declaration are taken from the *Book of Services*. The United Methodist Publishing House, 1985, p. 58. Originally appearing in *From Ashes to Fire*. Copyright © 1979 Abingdon Press. Reprinted by permission. The second declaration is adapted by permission from *Book of Worship: United Church of Christ*. Copyright 1986 United Church of Christ Office for Church Life and Leadership, p. 143.

[11]The first two prayers are adapted by permission from *Book of Worship: United Church of Christ*. Copyright 1986 United Church of Christ Office for Church Life and Leadership, p. 143f. The third prayer ("Merciful God...") is

taken from *Holy Baptism and Services for the Renewal of Baptism: The Worship of God (Supplemental Liturgical Resource 2)*, p. 42. Copyright © 1985 Westminster Press. Used by permission of Westminster/John Knox Press.

[12]See note 7.

[13]See note 8.

[14]Clark M. Williamson. *Baptism: Embodiment of the Gospel*. Christian Board of Publication, 1987, p. 36.

[15]*Ibid.*, p. 39.

[16]Insights in this paragraph were suggested by Martha Grace Reese.

[17]The first of these prayers is adapted from the *Book of Common Prayer* (reprinted by permission of HarperCollins Publishers Inc.) and the other prayers were written by LaTaunya M. Bynum.

[18]Adapted from *The Alternate Service Book 1980*. Cambridge University Press, p. 322f. Copyright © The Central Board of Finance of the Church of England. The psalm is reprinted with permission from its original location in *The Psalms: A New Translation for Worship*, HarperCollins Publishers Inc.

[19]See note 8.

[20]This prayer is adapted from *Pastoral Care of the Sick: Rites of Anointing and Viaticum*. International Commission on English in the Liturgy, 1982, p. 97. All rights reserved.

[21]Adapted from *Holy Baptism and Services for the Renewal of Baptism: The Worship of God (Supplemental Liturgical Resource 2)*, p. 33f. Copyright © 1985 Westminster Press. Used by permission of Westminster/John Knox Press.

[22]Adapted by permission from *Book of Worship: United Church of Christ*. Copyright 1986 United Church of Christ Office for Church Life and Leadership.

[23]The paschal candle is a large decorative candle used in the Easter Vigil. Traditionally, it is placed in a special stand near the communion table and lighted during worship each Sunday through the Day of Pentecost. It is then placed near the baptistry and lighted whenever baptisms are performed. The candle should be at least two inches in diameter and two feet in height. These candles have traditionally been inscribed with a cross, the Greek letters alpha and omega, and the numerals of the current year. See *United Methodist Altars: A Guide for the Local Church*, by Hoyt L. Hickman. Abingdon Press, 1984, p. 53.

[24]Adapted from *Thankful Praise*, edited by Keith Watkins. CBP Press, 1987, p. 104f.

[25]This service is adapted from *Worship for the Way*. The Board of Congregational Life, The Presbyterian Church in Canada, 1988, pp. 10-15. Used by permission.

[26]This order is adapted from *An Order of Thanksgiving for the Birth or Adoption of a Child*. The Consultation on Church Union, 1980, pp. 10-14.

[27]This service is revised from *An Affirmation of the Baptismal Covenant*. The Consultation on Church Union, 1990, pp. 7-11.

[28]See note 7.

[29]See note 8.

[30]Marion J. Hatchett, *Commentary on the American Prayer Book*. Seabury Press, 1981, p. 239f.

[31]Saint Basil of Caesarea, Baptismal Homilies, in Edward Yarnold's *The Awe Inspiring Rites of Initiation: Baptismal Homilies of the Fourth Century*. St. Pauls, 1976.

[32]Justin Martyr, *The First Apology*, translated by Thomas B. Falls. Christian Heritage, 1948, p. 99.

[33]*The Apostolic Tradition of Hippolytus*, translated by Burton Scott Easton. Cambridge University Press, 1934, p. 44.

[34]*Ibid.*, p. 44f.
[35]Alexander Campbell, "Positive Christian Institutions." *Millennial Harbinger*, Vol. 32, p. 250.
[36]*Ibid.*, p. 247.